AF255484

Living with Pottery

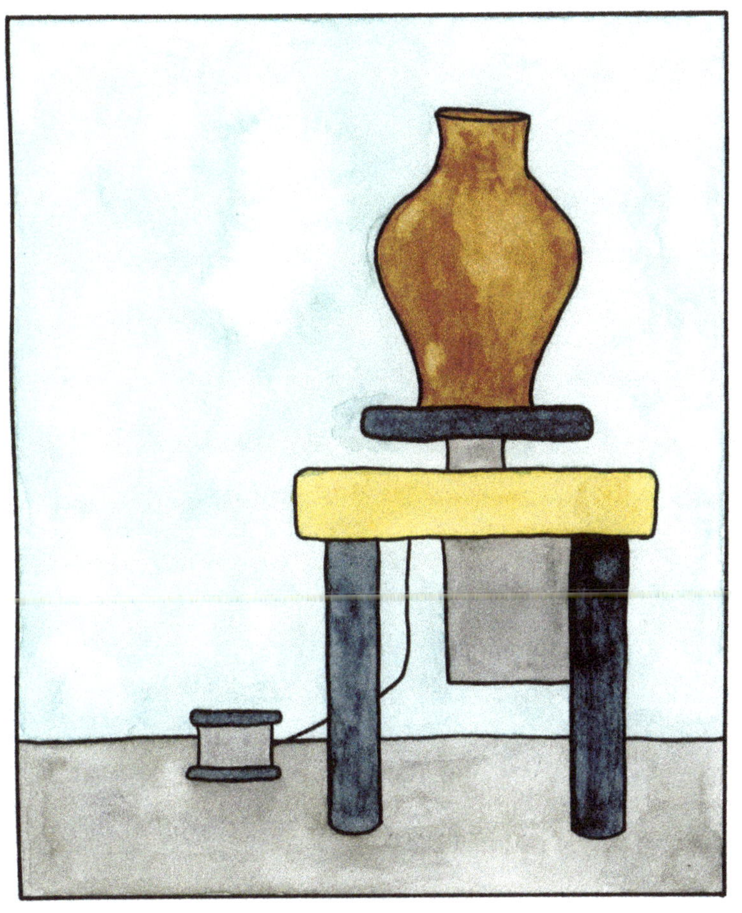

Justine Riley

Text set in InkFree

Summary: A lyrical depiction of pottery in the home and a glimpse into the practice of potters.

Special thanks to Debi Danielson

"We hold each other's histories." These exact words came to me days after the death of Joy Thomas. Peoms, paintings and pottery these are some of the many places I find Joy.

Digital design by Josh Riley

ISBN 978-1-17323083-3-6

Published by Sketch • Journal • Record

www.SketchJournalRecord.com

Mayfield, KY

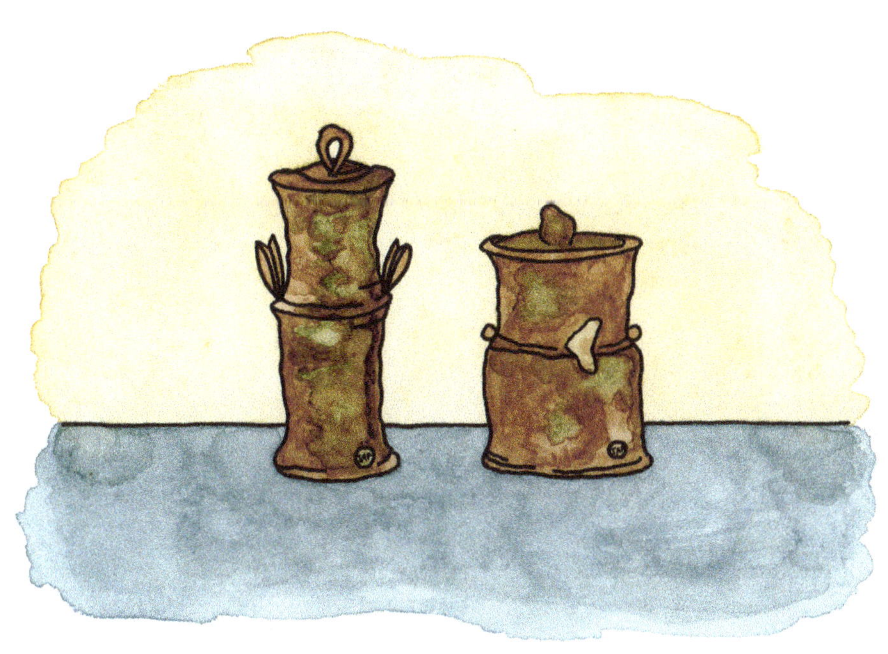

to Josh Riley
my partner in crime
we need a larger mug shelf

to the clay community
where my artistic path began

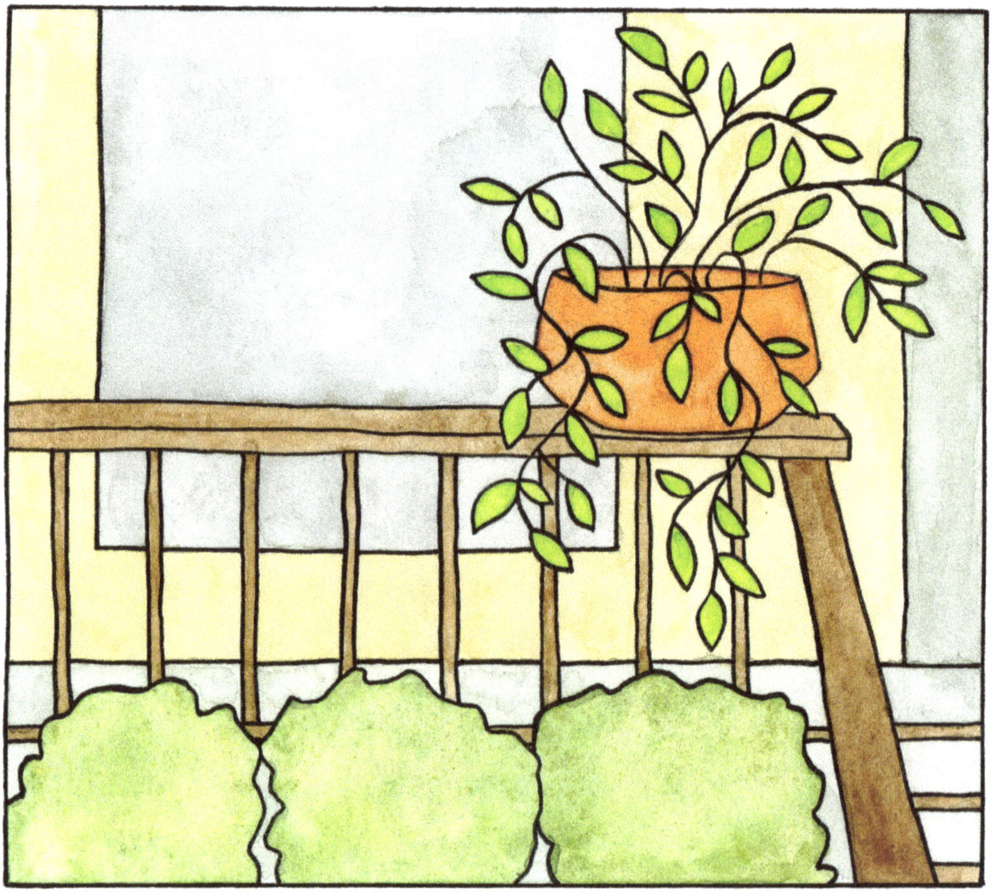

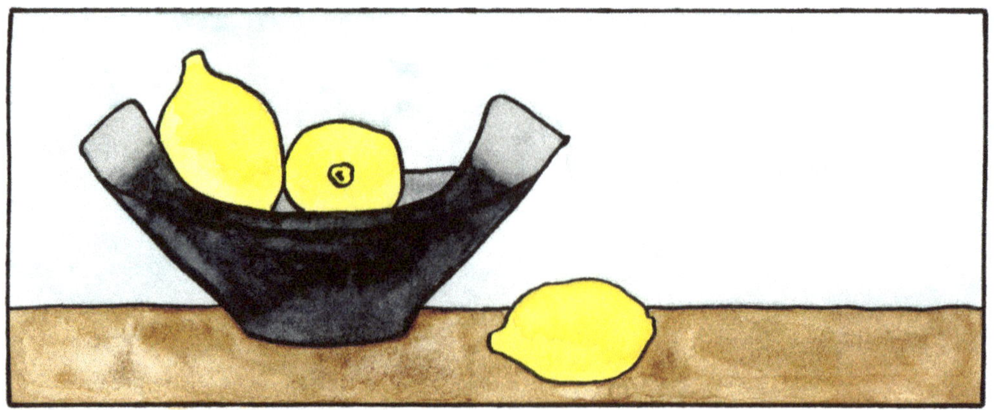

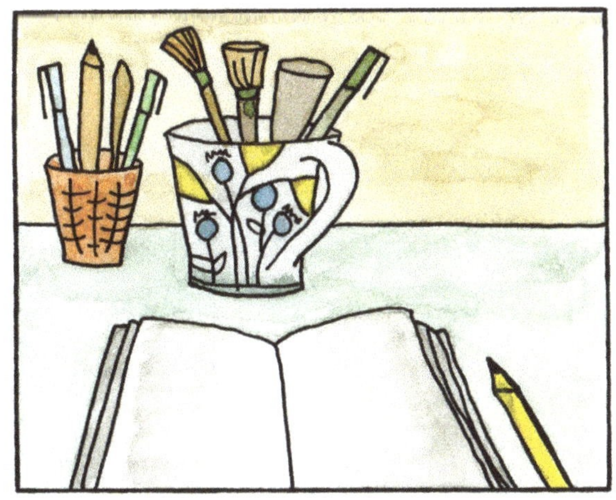

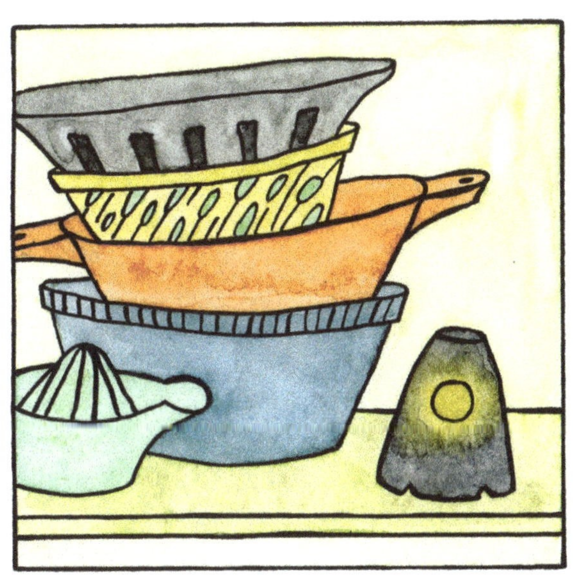

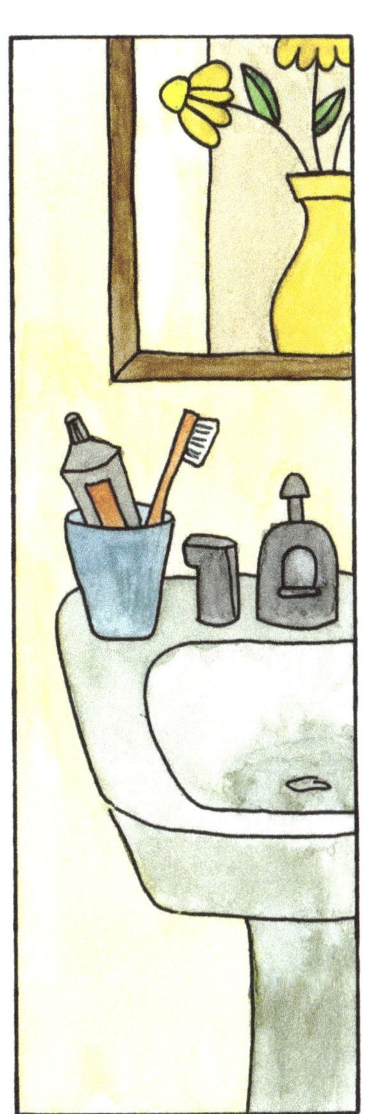

Pottery is quite nice.

Pots make everyday living more beautiful.

Pottery helps make a house a home.

The home - a living gallery.

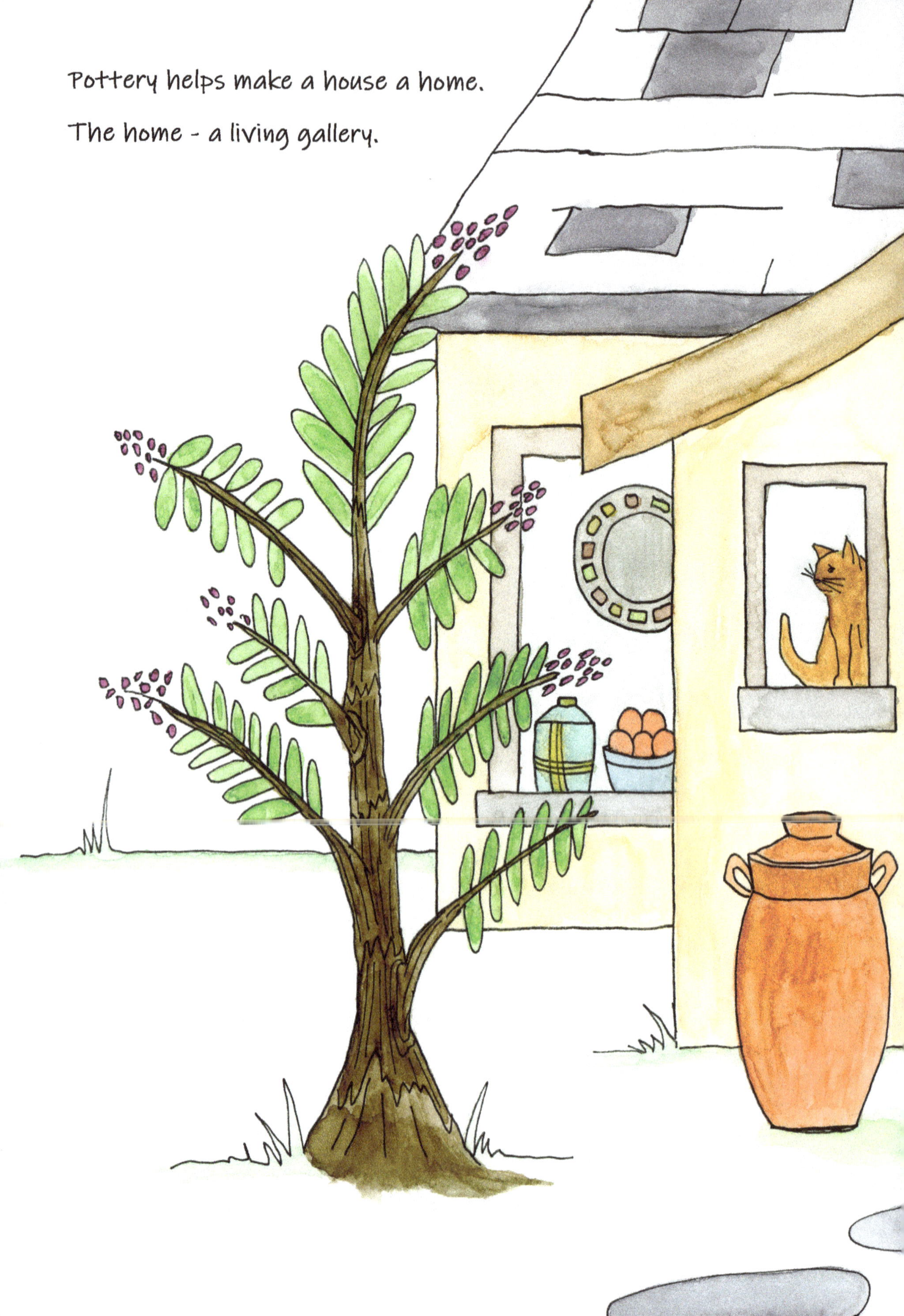

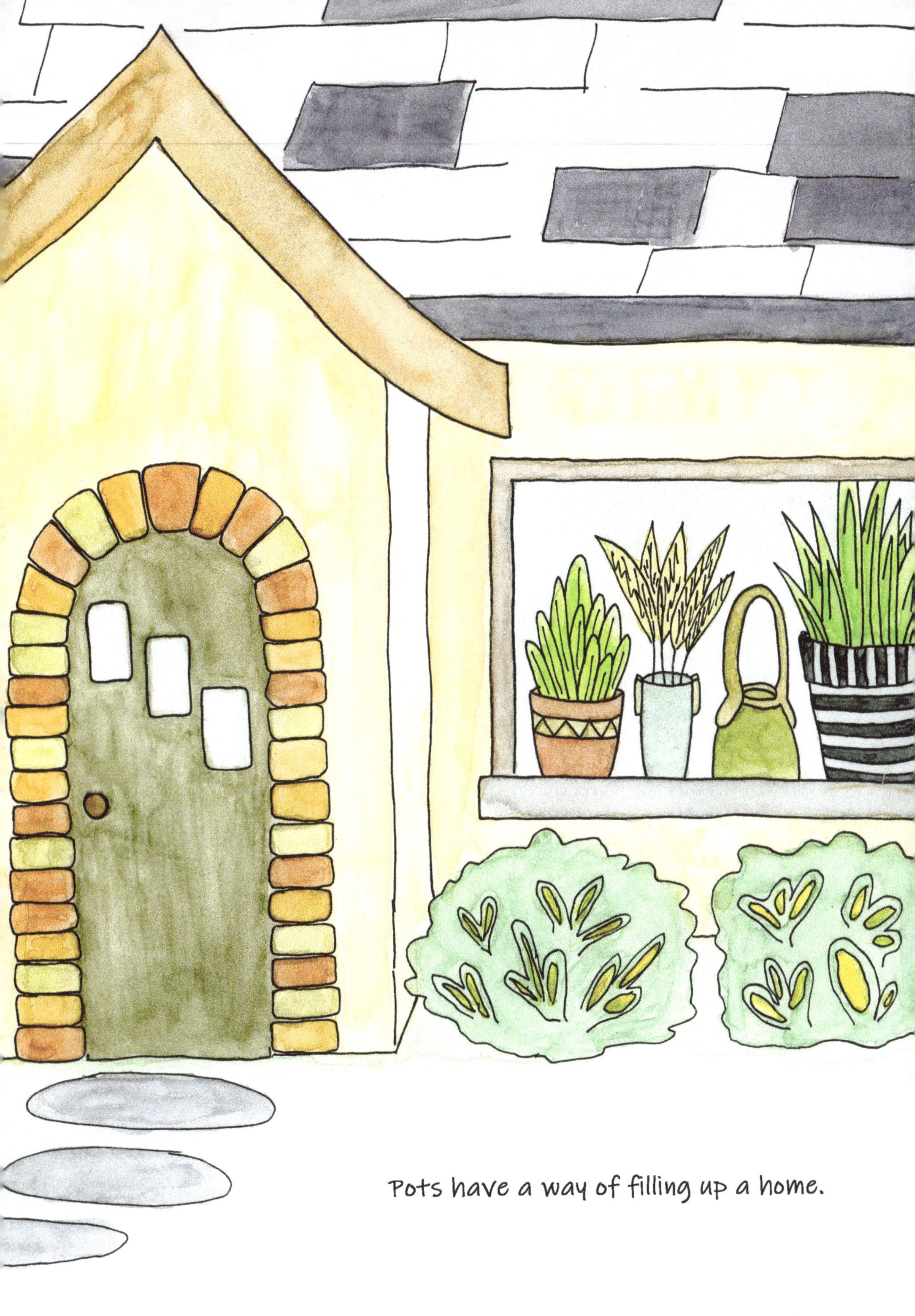

Pots have a way of filling up a home.

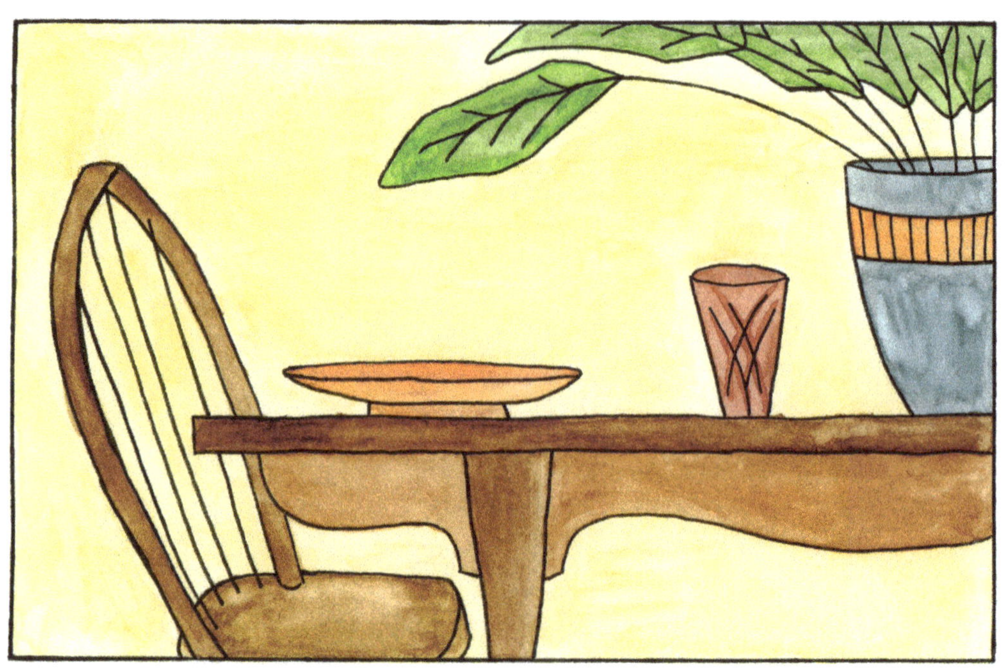

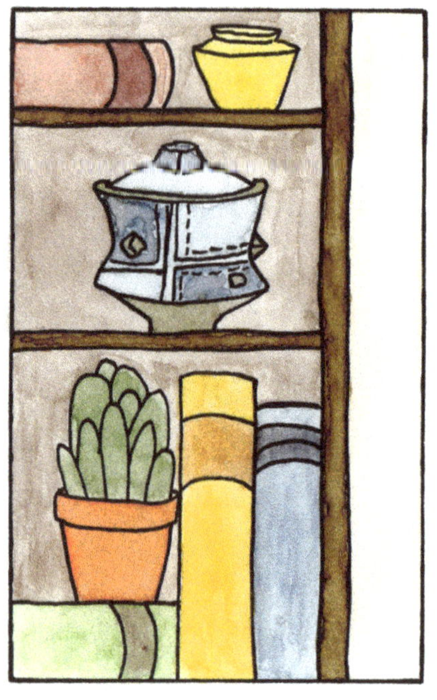

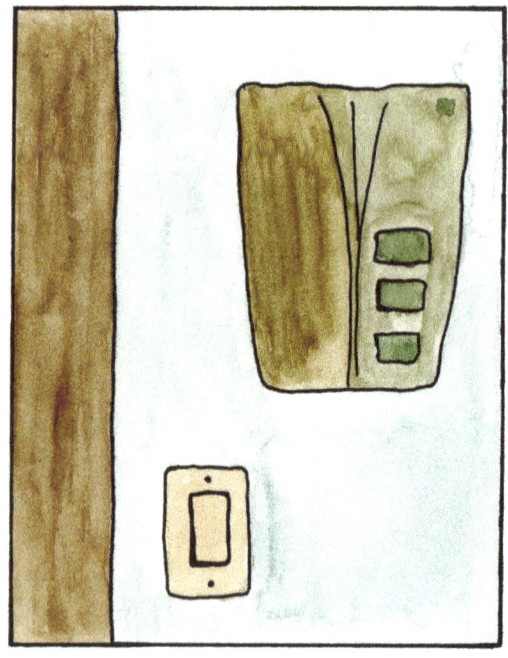

Pots live on shelves.

They visit tables

and hang on walls.

Pots rest on windowsills.

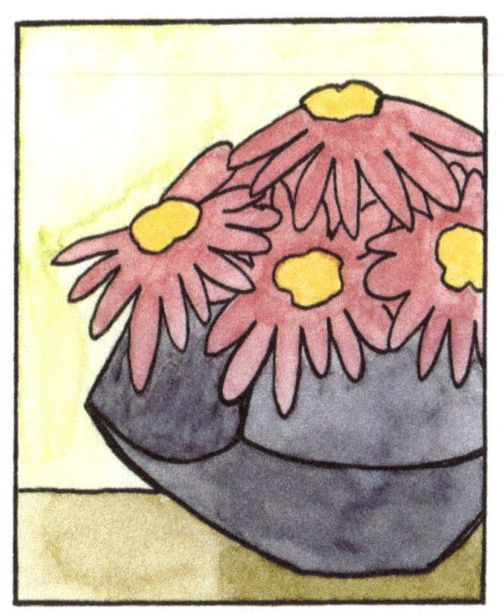

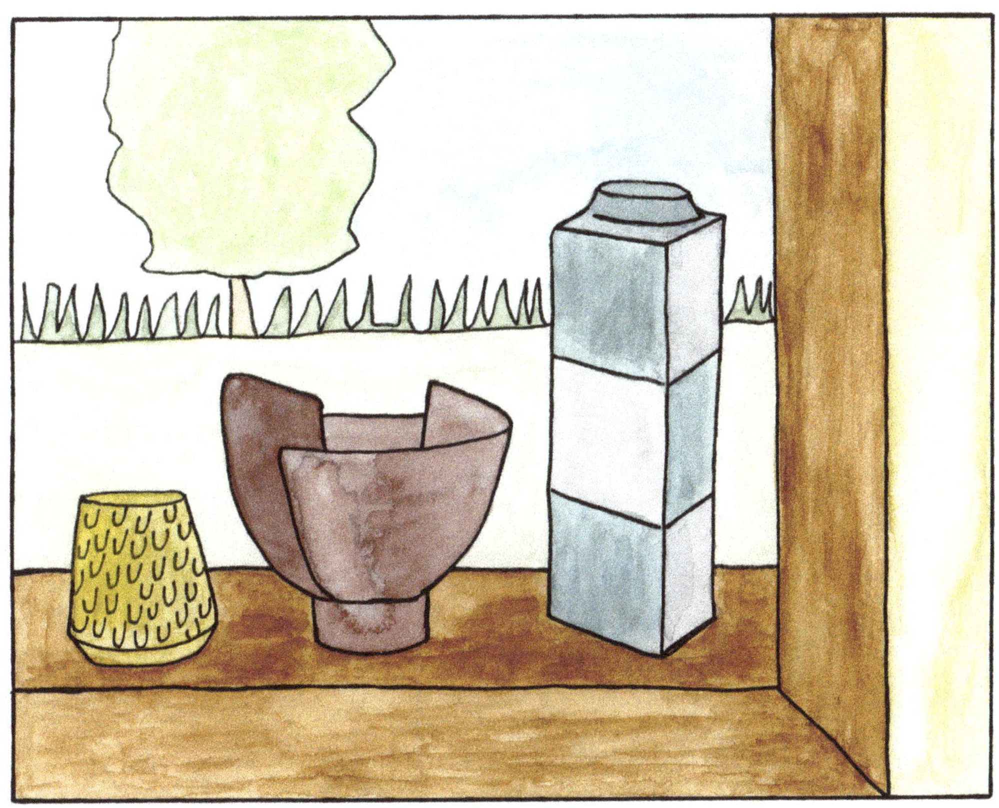

The pots on shelves,

they squeeze in tight

like passengers on the subway.

RUSH HOUR!

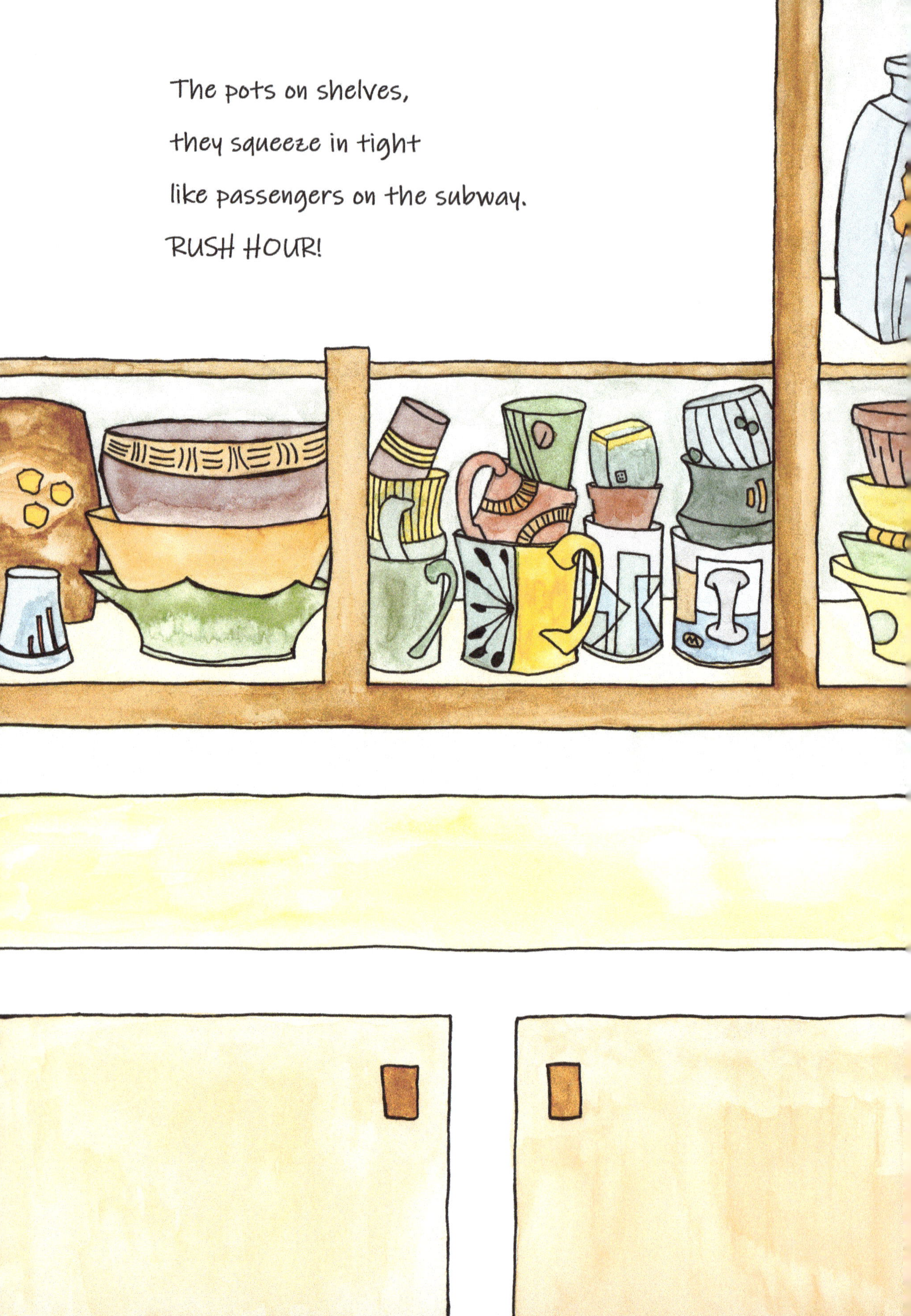

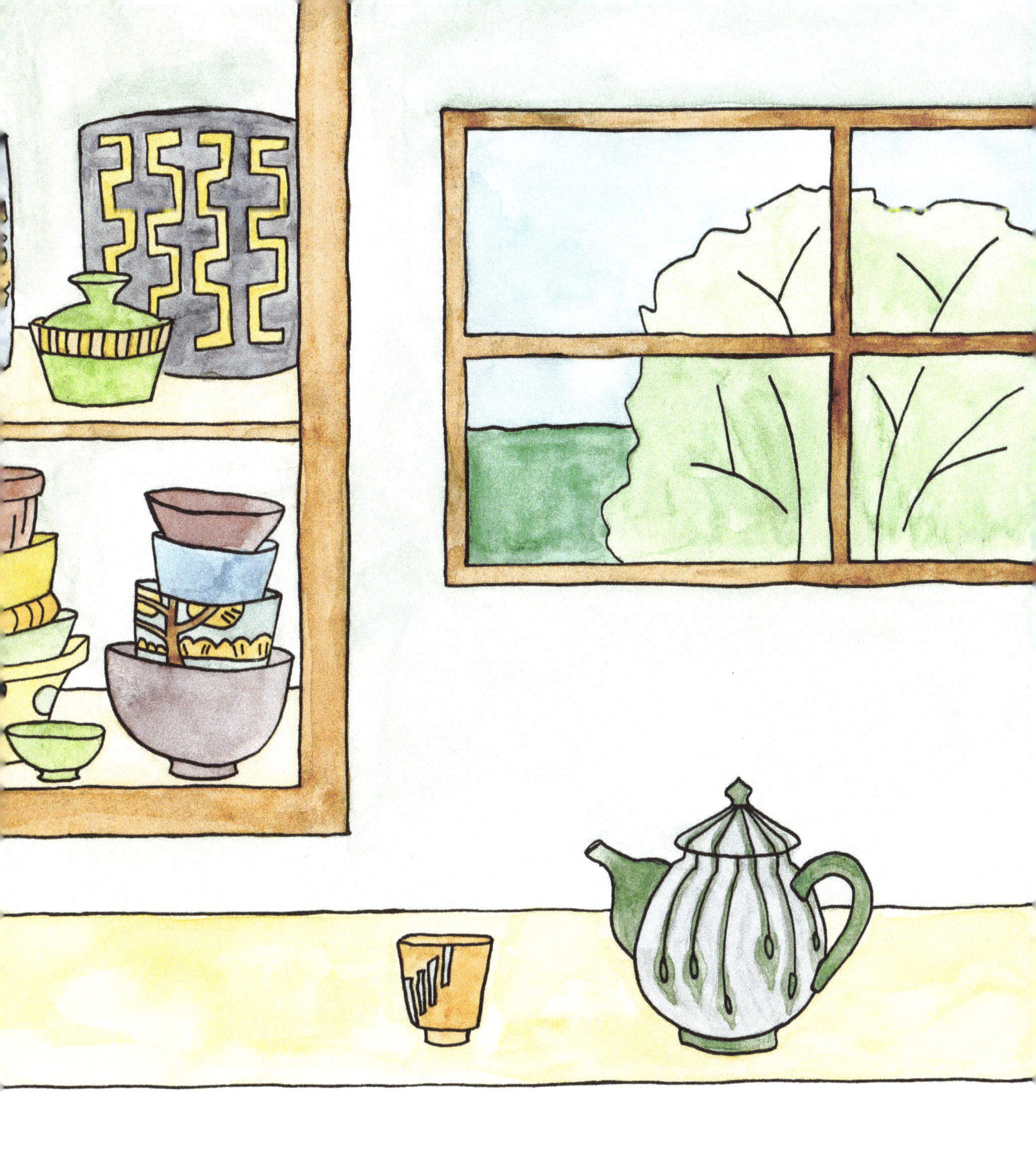

But the pots aren't going anywhere.

They are waiting,

waiting for their chance to be held,

to be filled, to be of service

yet again...

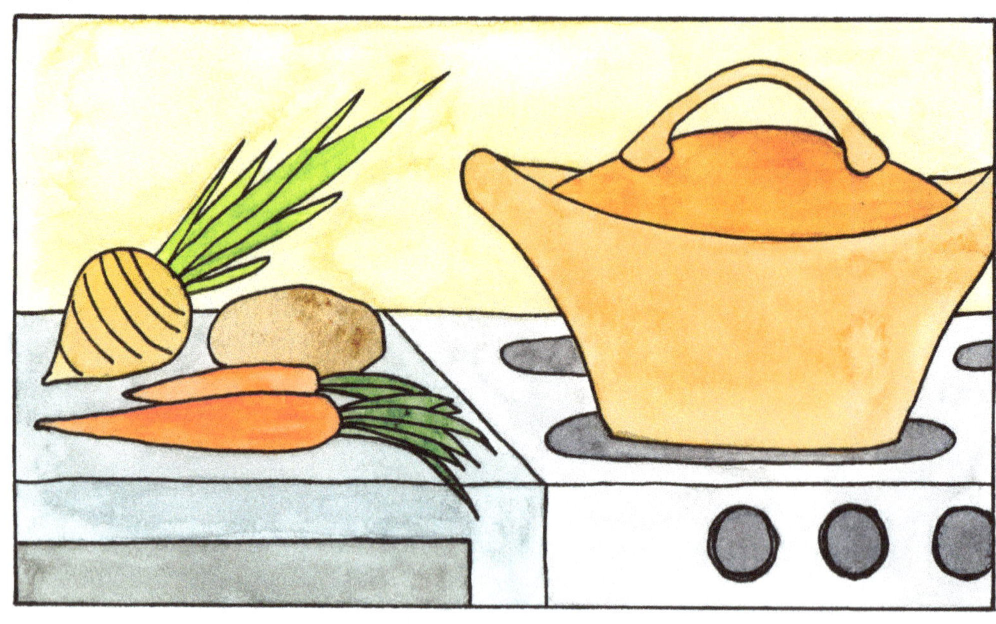

There are pots for pouring,

sipping and slurping.

There are pies in pots

and cookies too,

fermenting pots

and pots bubbling with stew.

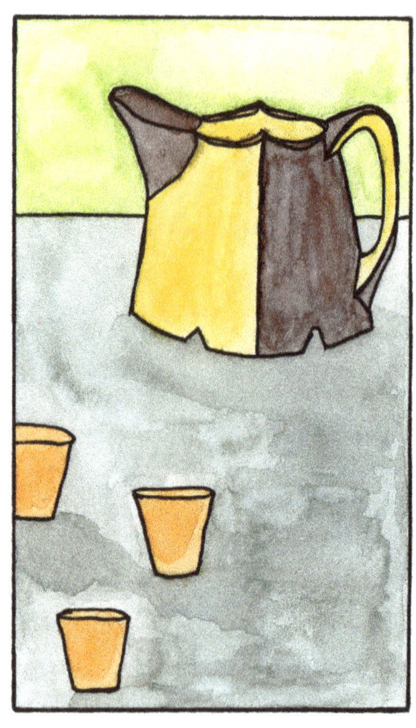

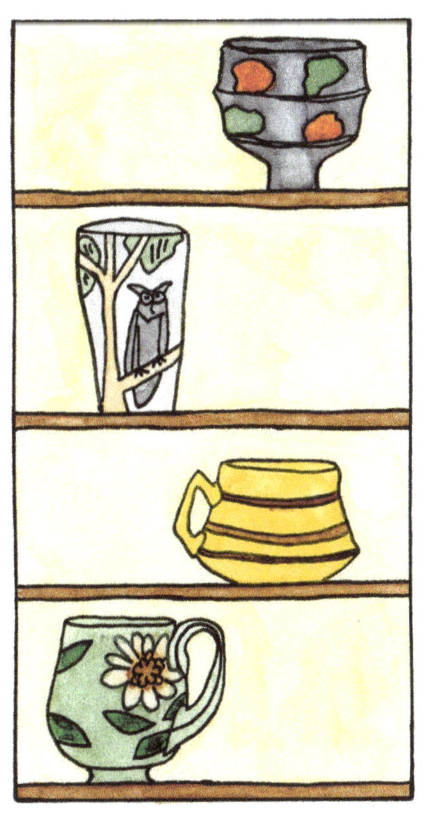

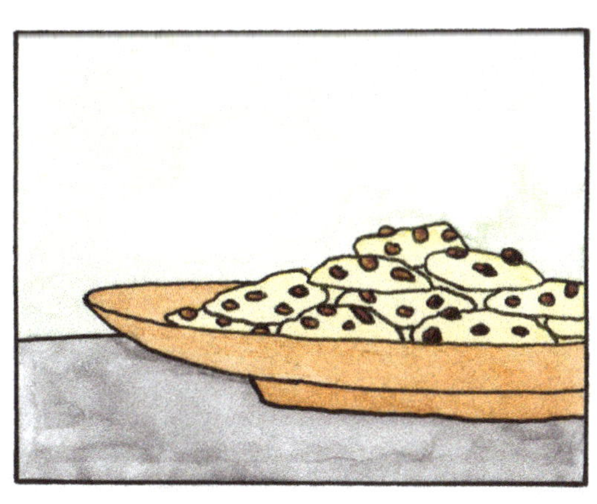

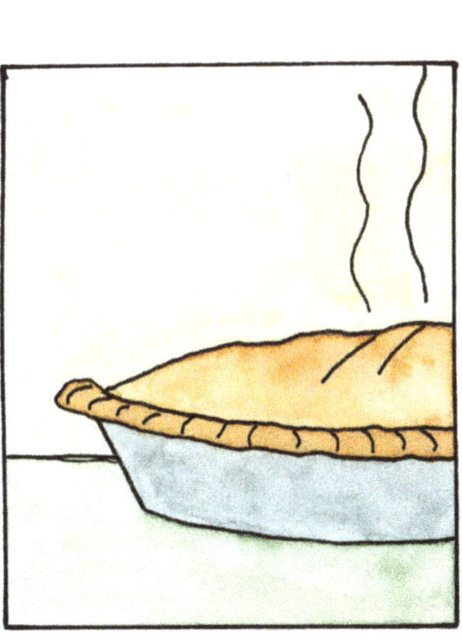

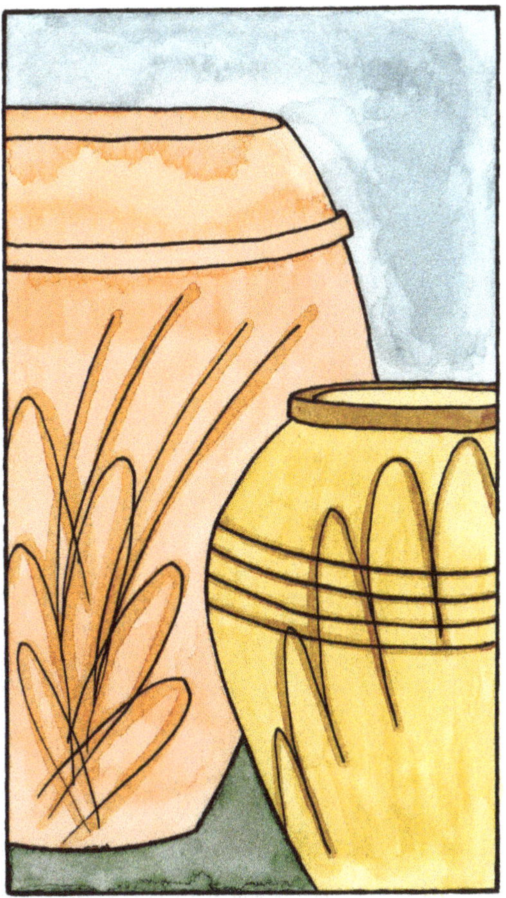

Pottery is nice to set a table with.

A chorus of voices joining together,

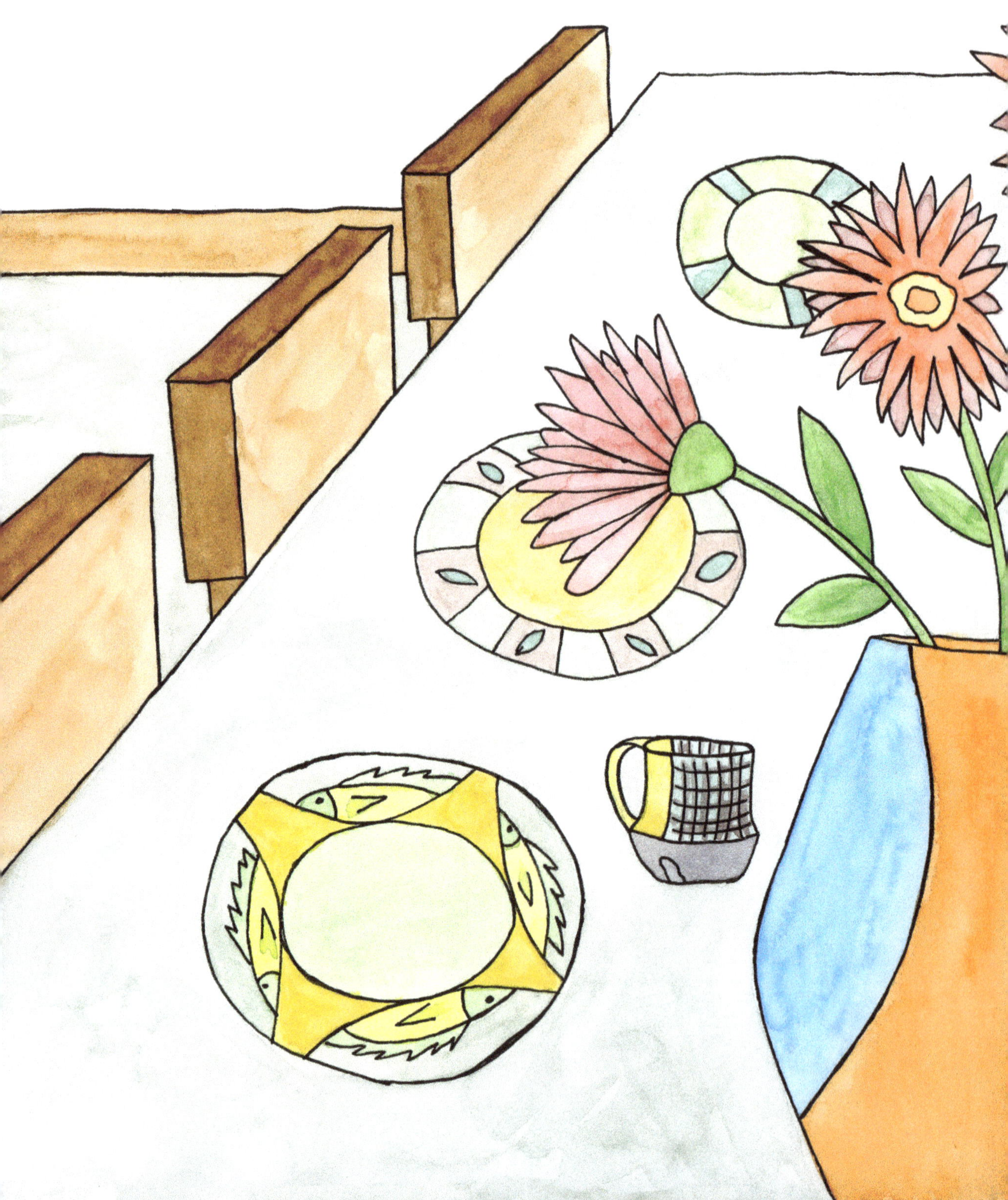

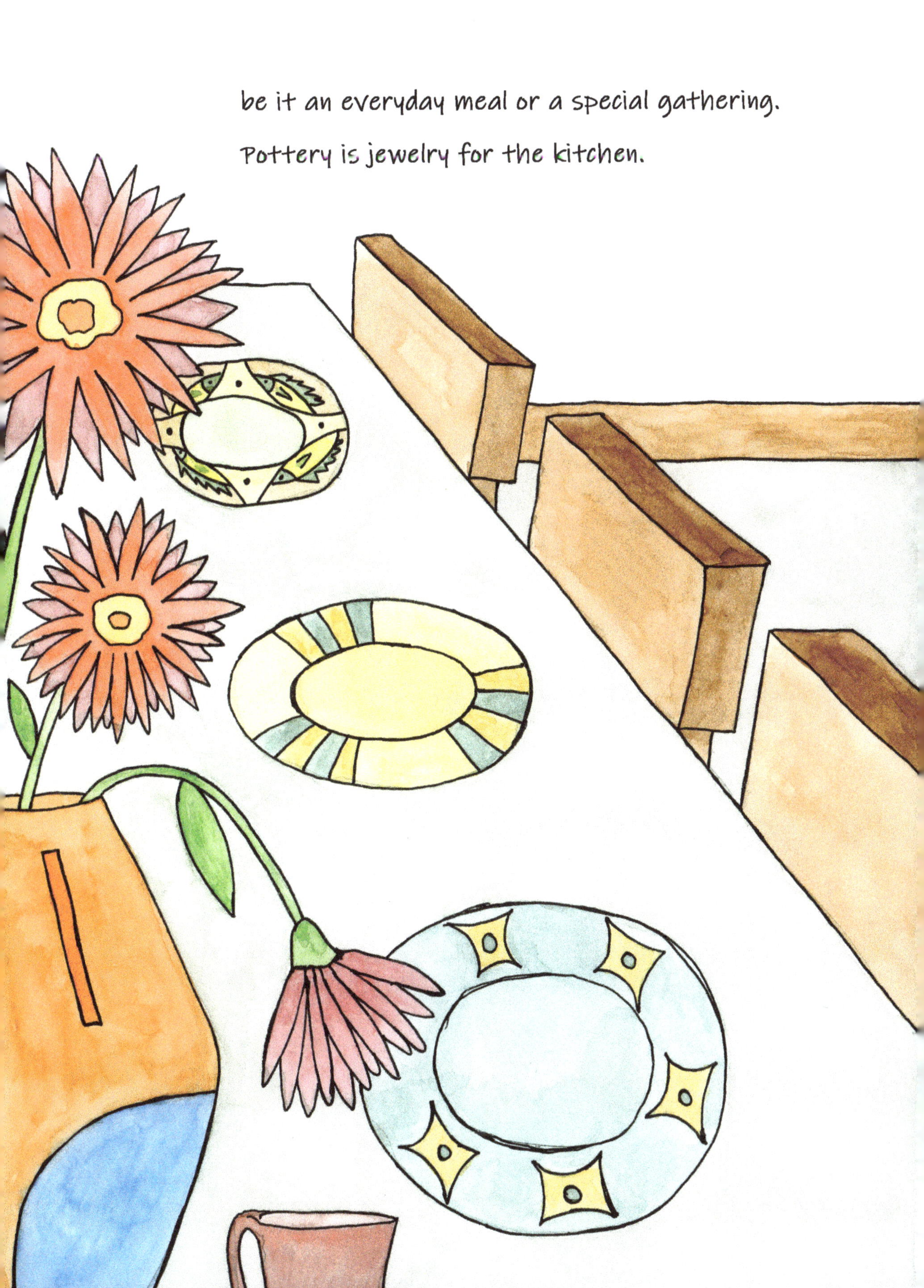
be it an everyday meal or a special gathering.
Pottery is jewelry for the kitchen.

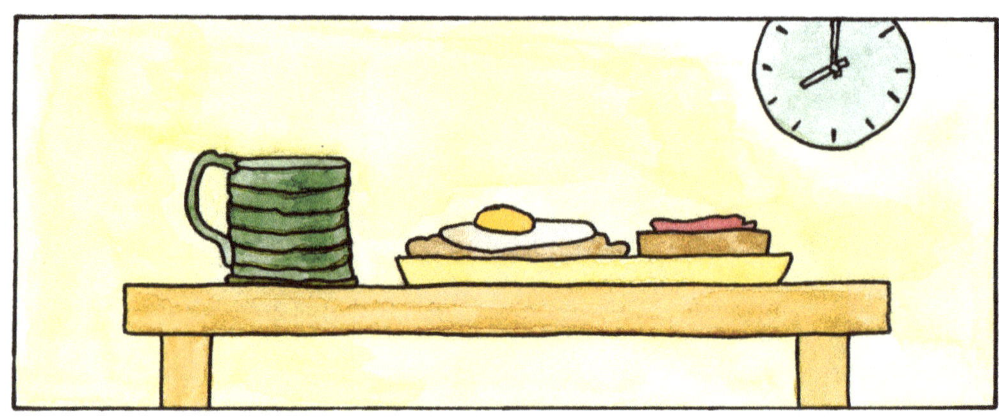

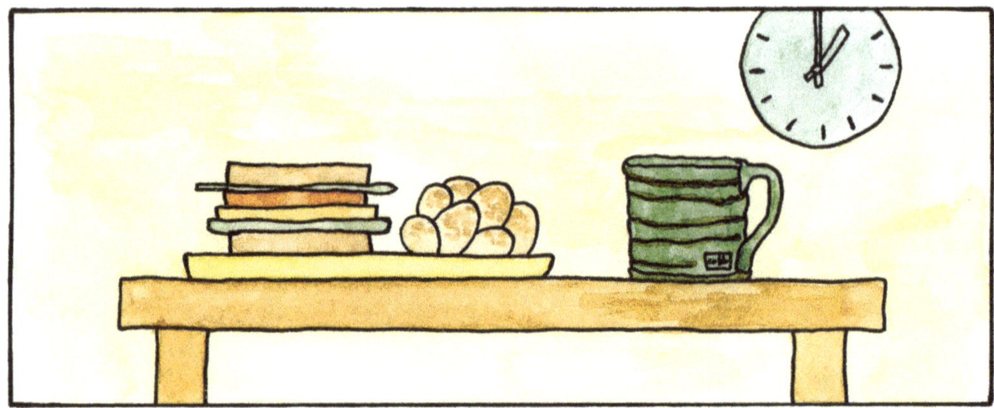

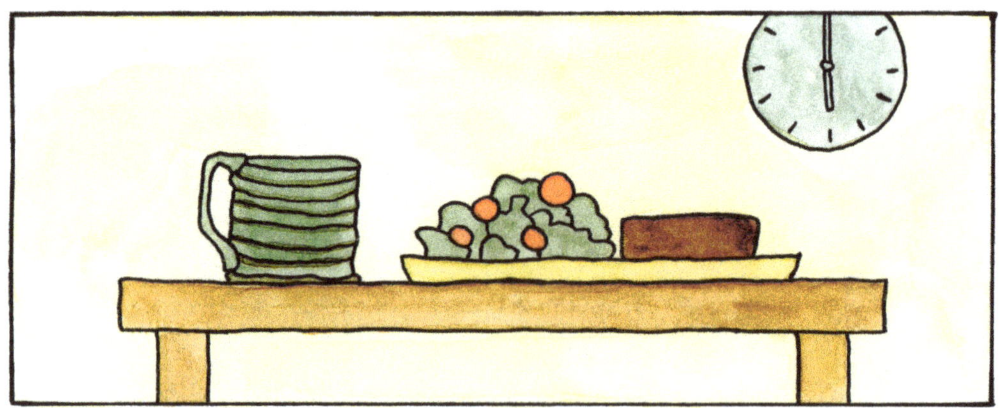

You might have just one pot
and that can be grand!
Use it three times a day
so you wash it by hand.

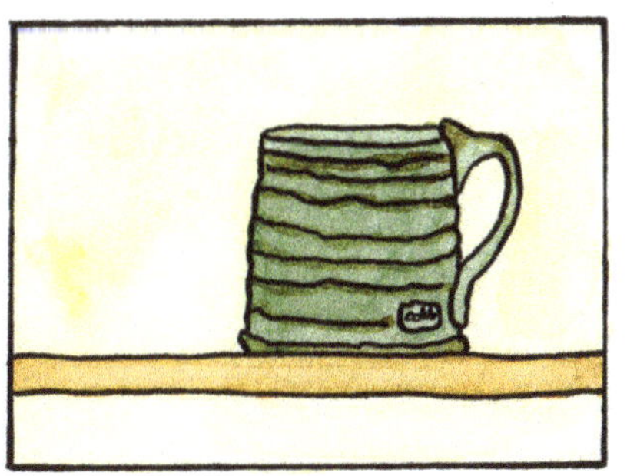

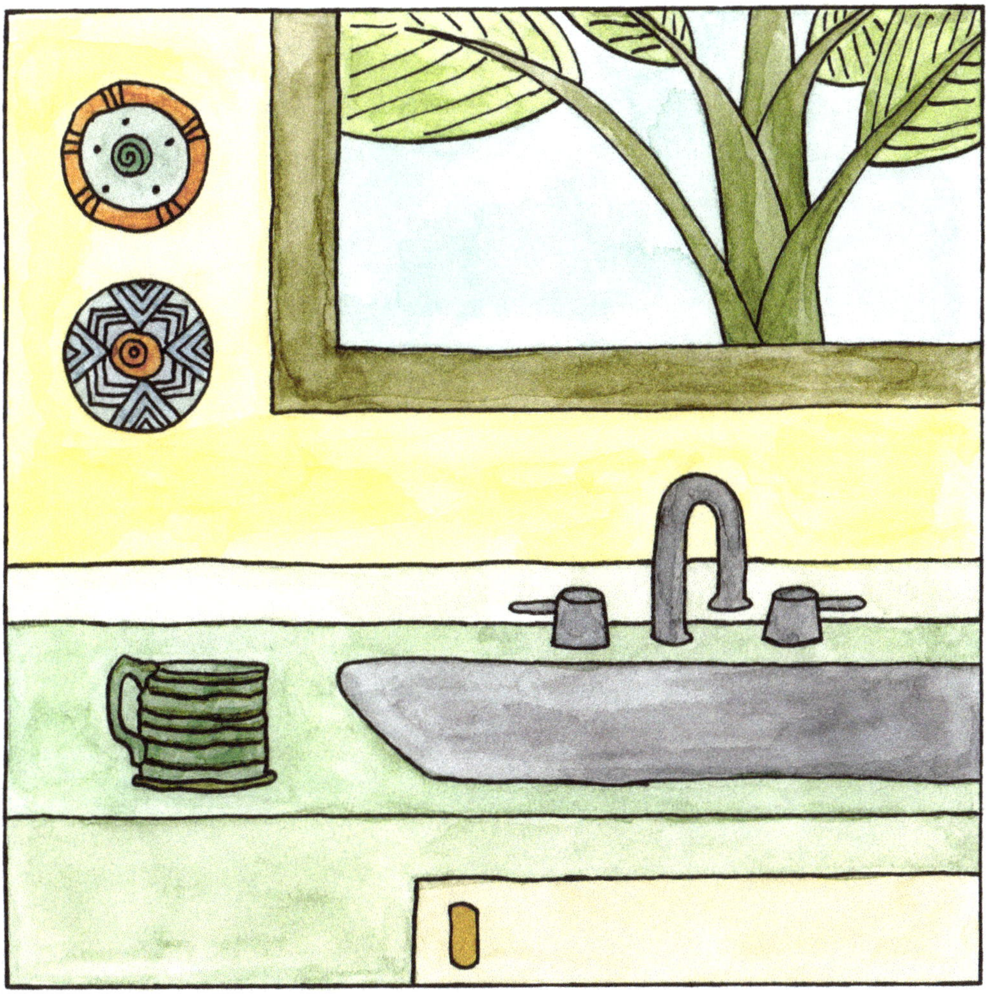

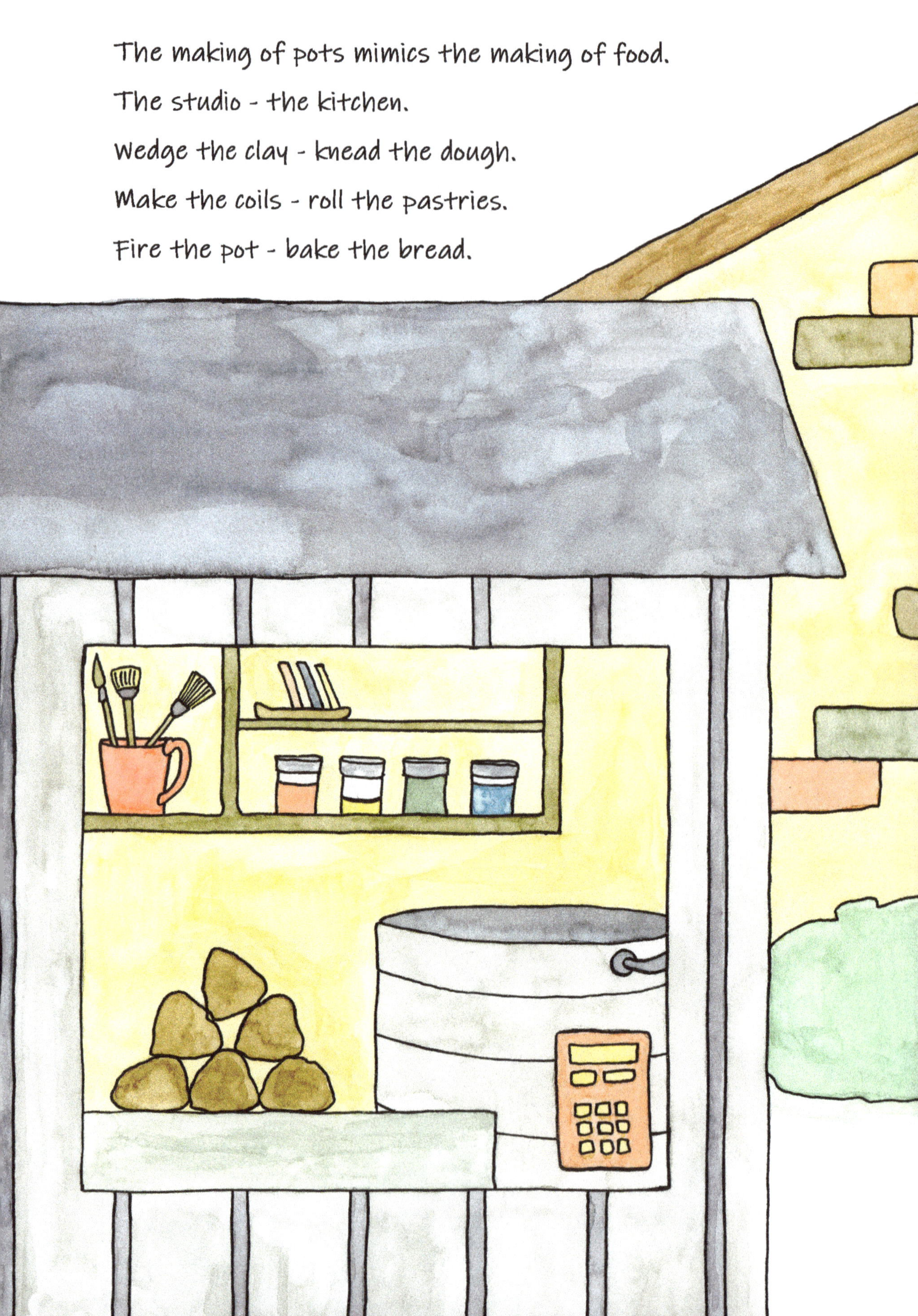

The making of pots mimics the making of food.
The studio - the kitchen.
Wedge the clay - knead the dough.
Make the coils - roll the pastries.
Fire the pot - bake the bread.

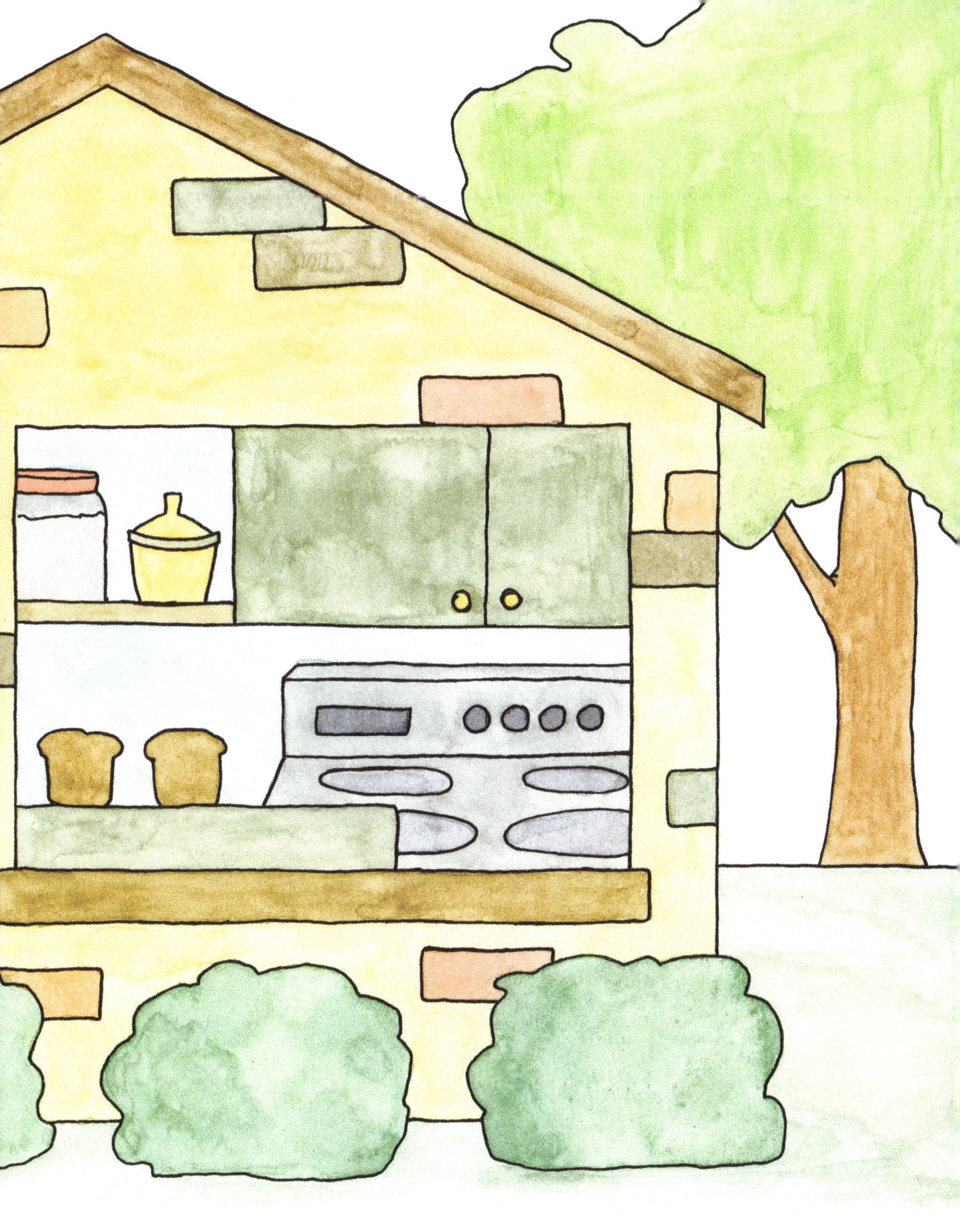

Both are forever changed and both become dishes.

A pot is nice to make.

An idea made by the hand

written in clay.

Then you can hold these ideas

and drink from them too.

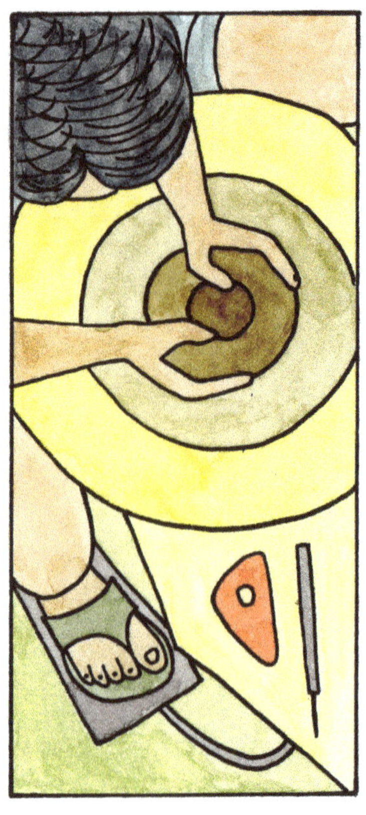

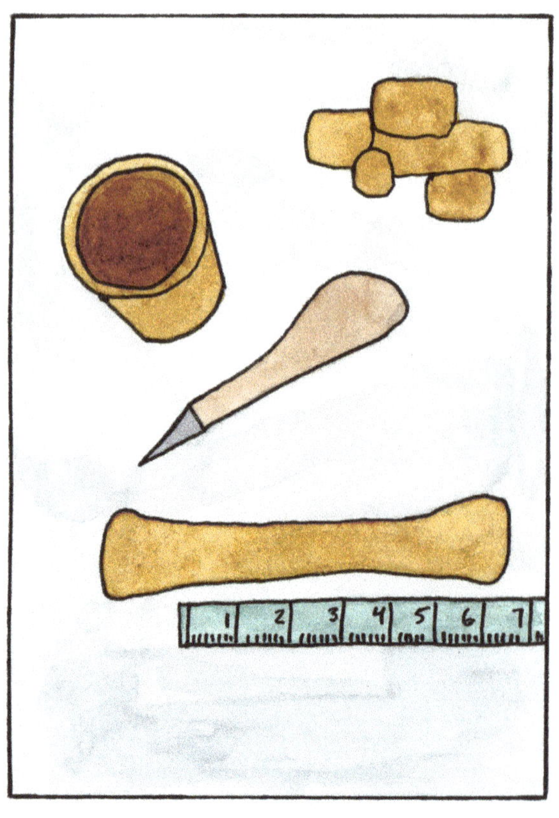

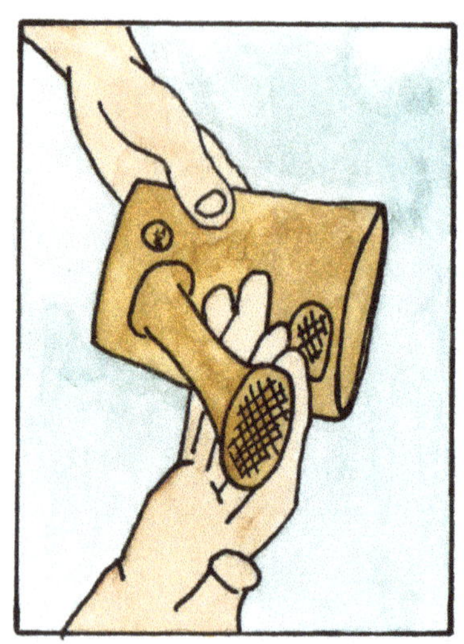

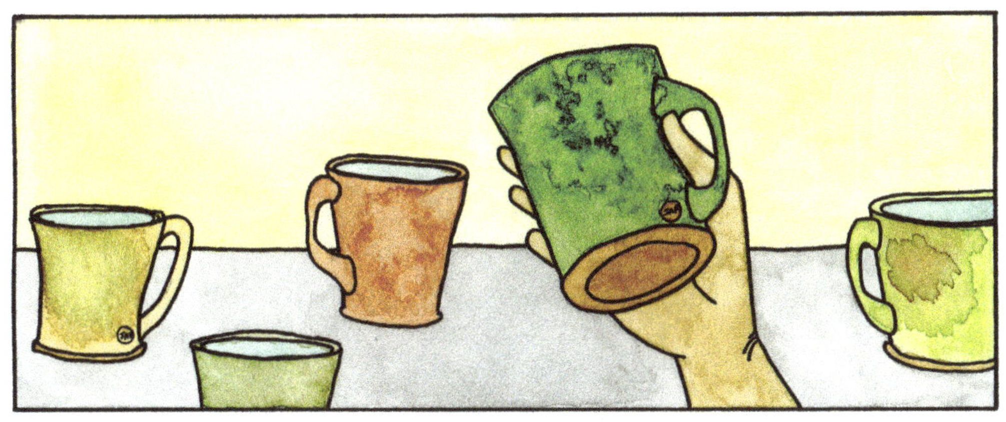

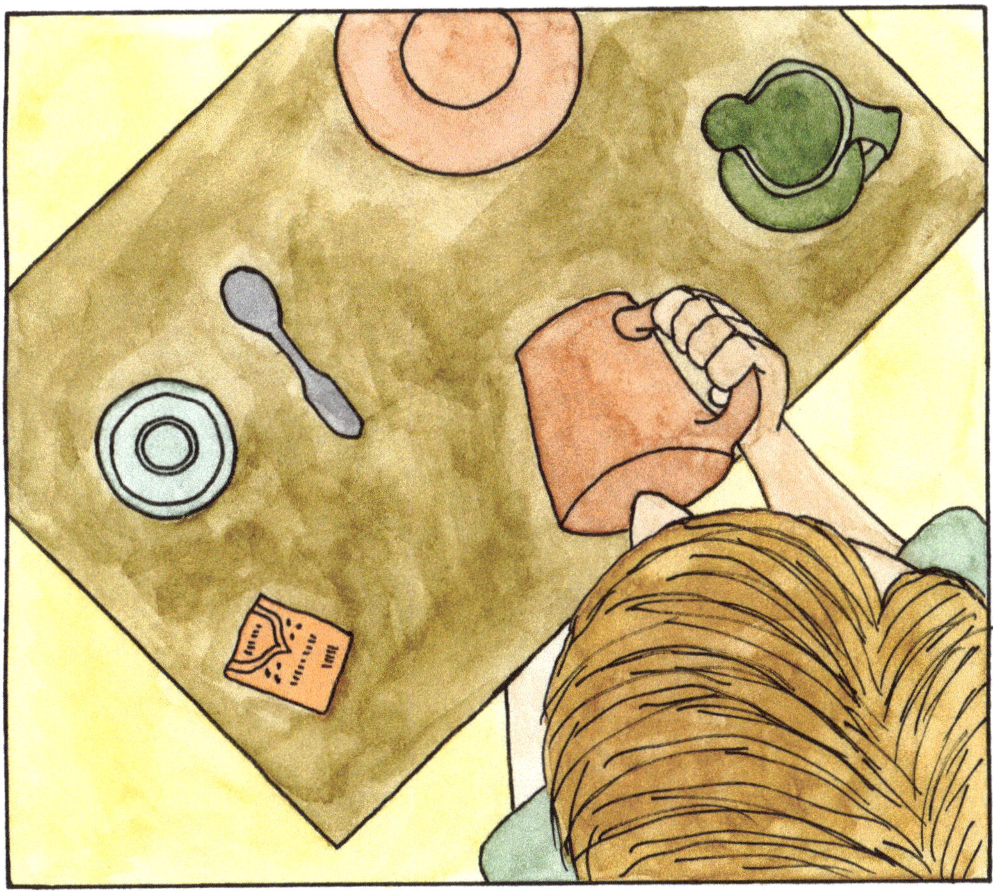

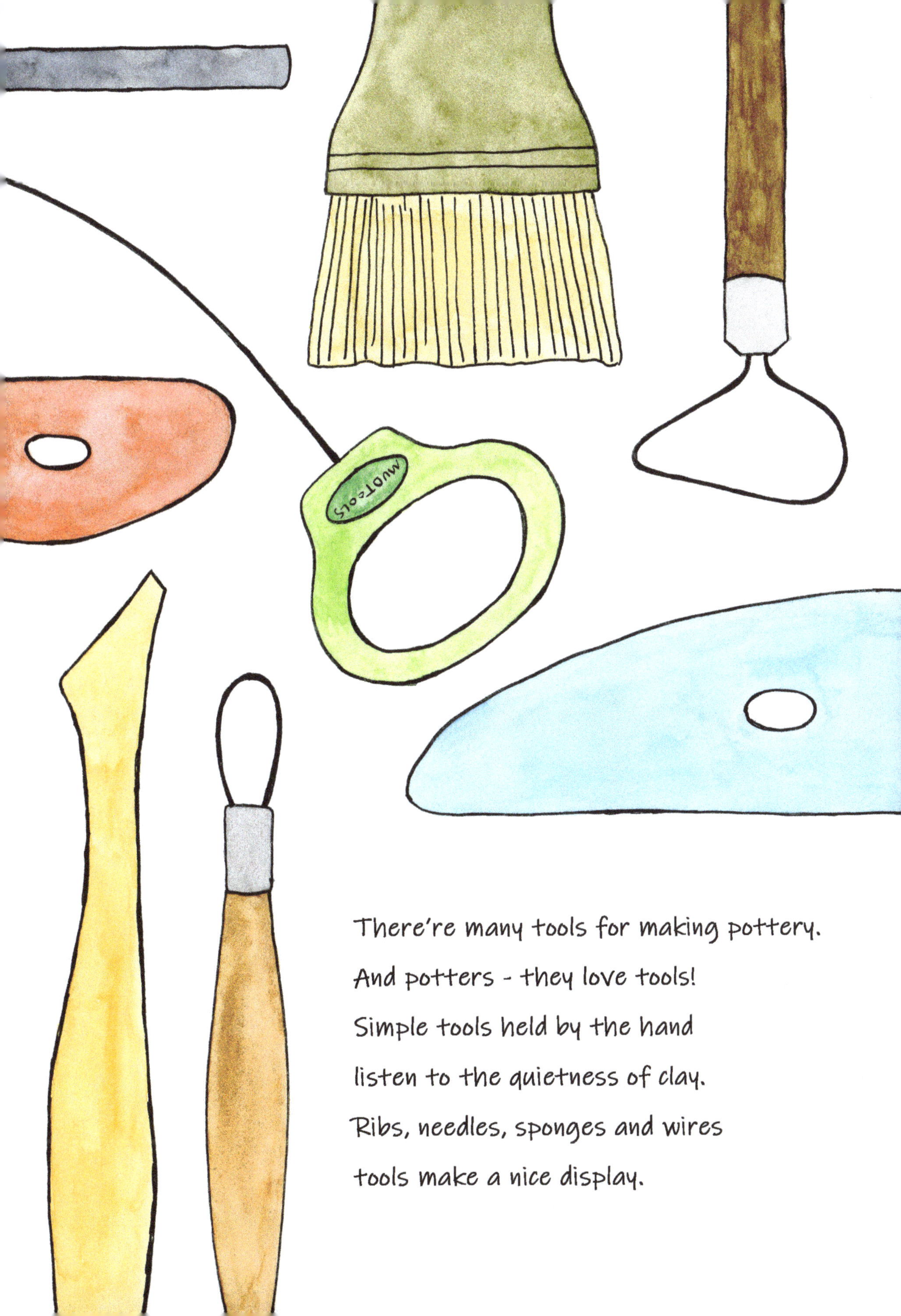

There're many tools for making pottery.
And potters - they love tools!
Simple tools held by the hand
listen to the quietness of clay.
Ribs, needles, sponges and wires
tools make a nice display.

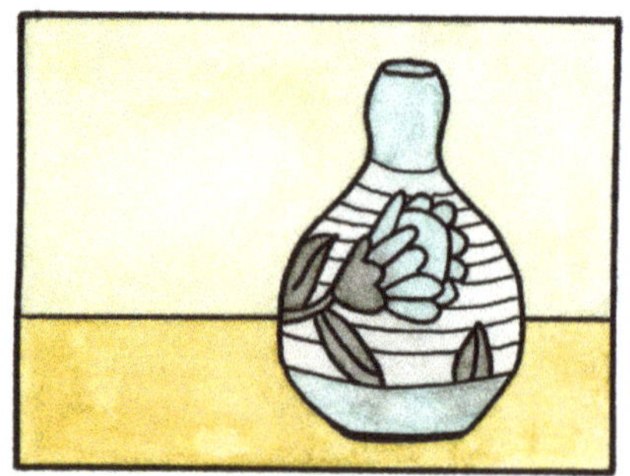

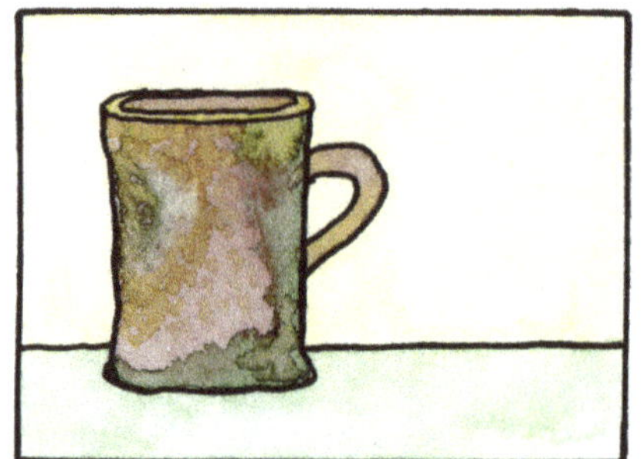

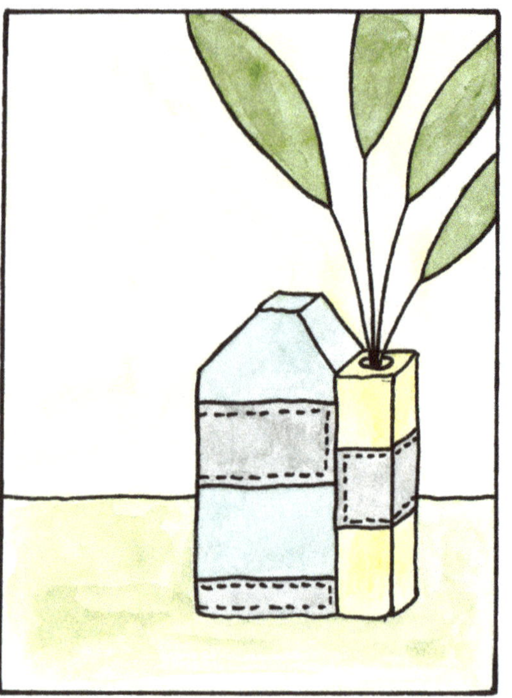

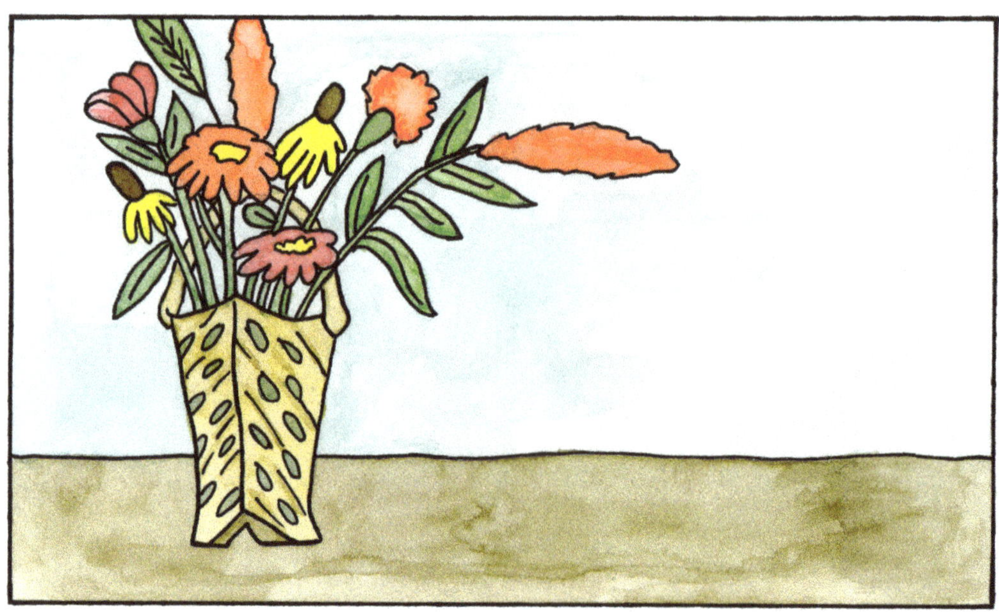

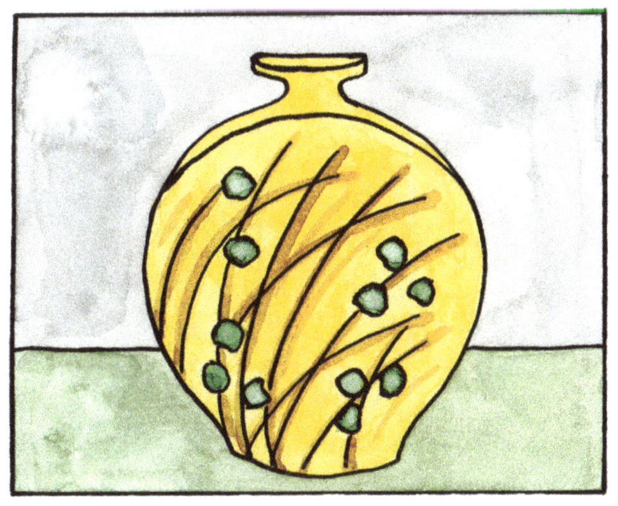

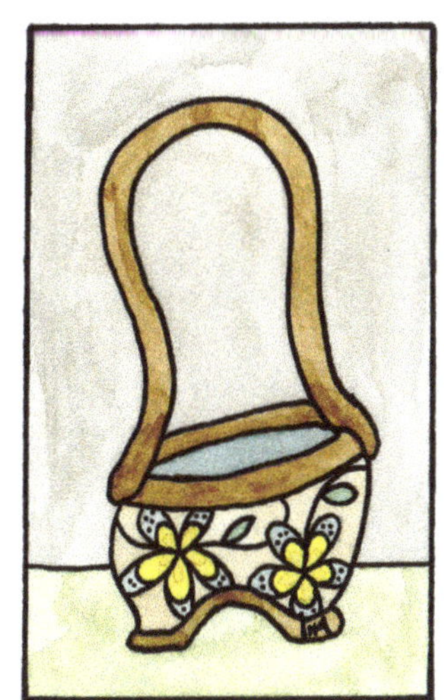

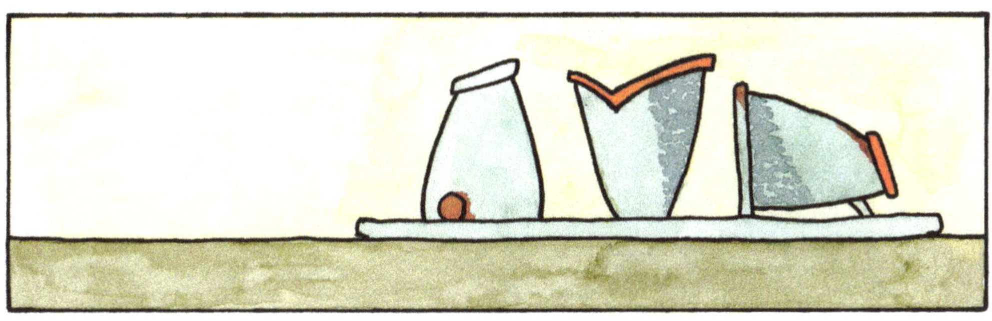

Living with pottery

is about living with people,

people who make pottery.

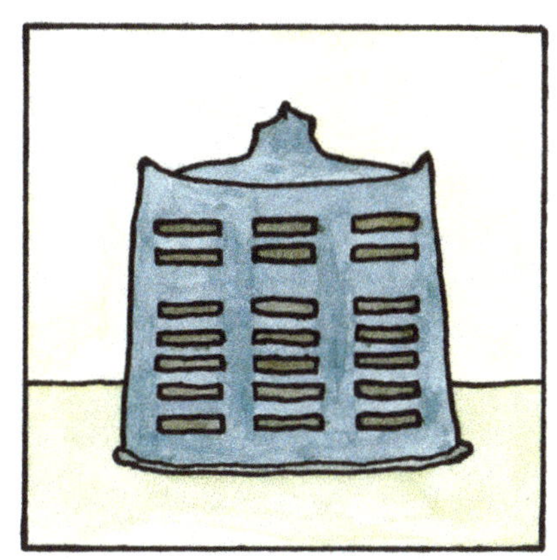

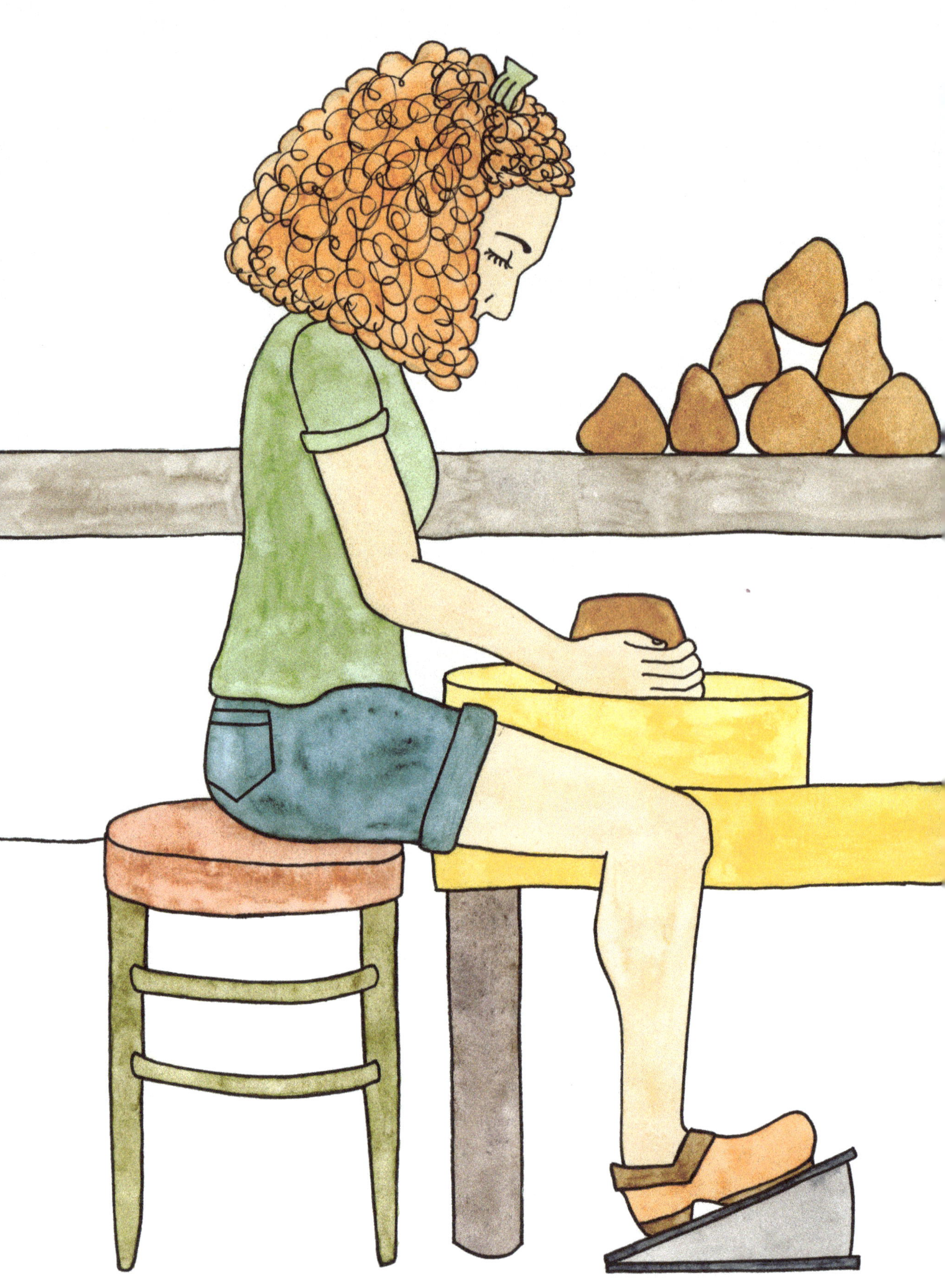

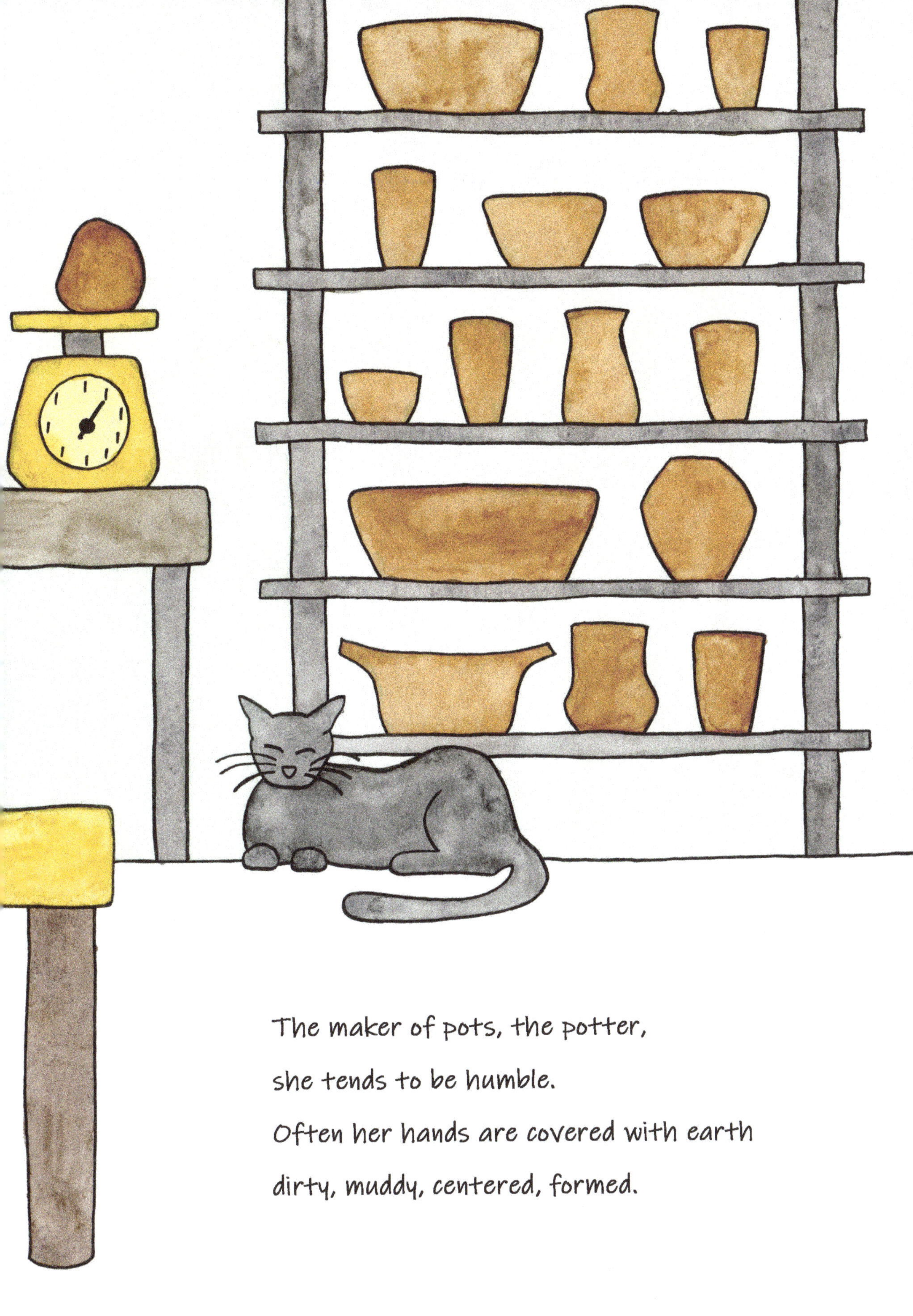

The maker of pots, the potter,

she tends to be humble.

Often her hands are covered with earth

dirty, muddy, centered, formed.

The potter breathes failure.

He moves quickly through broken,

fractured, poorly glazed and S cracked pots.

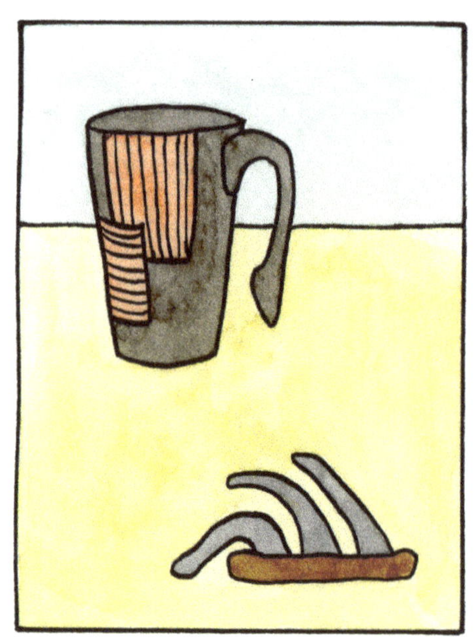

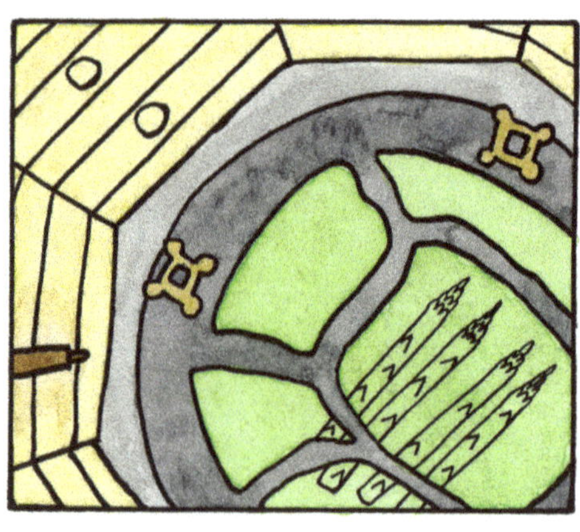

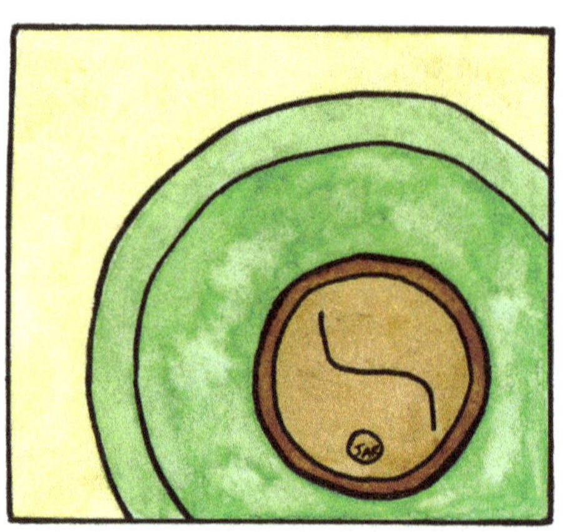

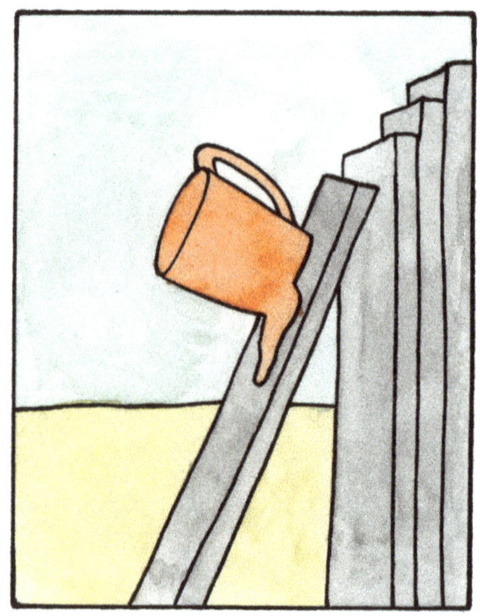

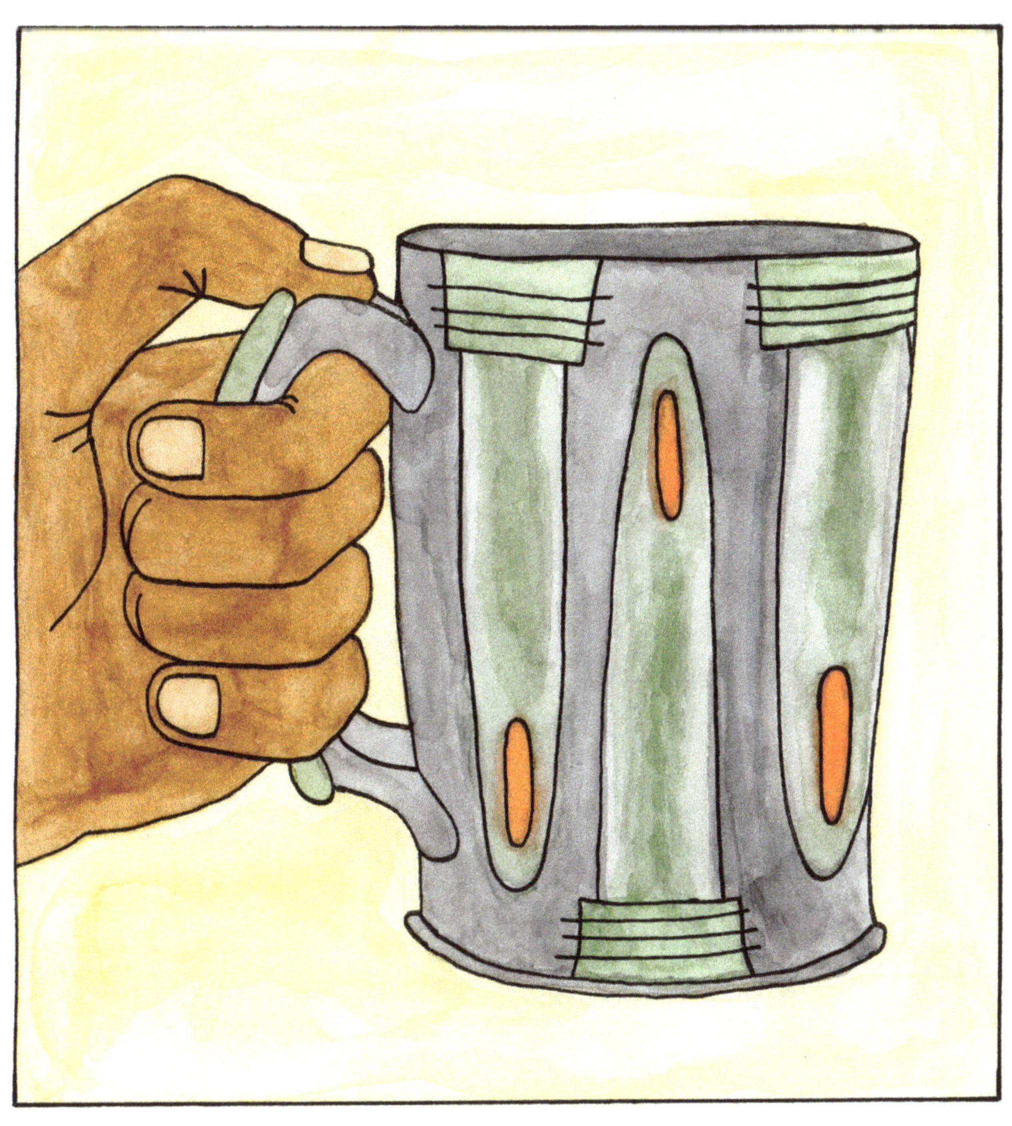

But the beauties, the eye-catchers, the stunners

these pots all have their piles of failures holding them up.

Living with these pots is living with the beauty of failure.

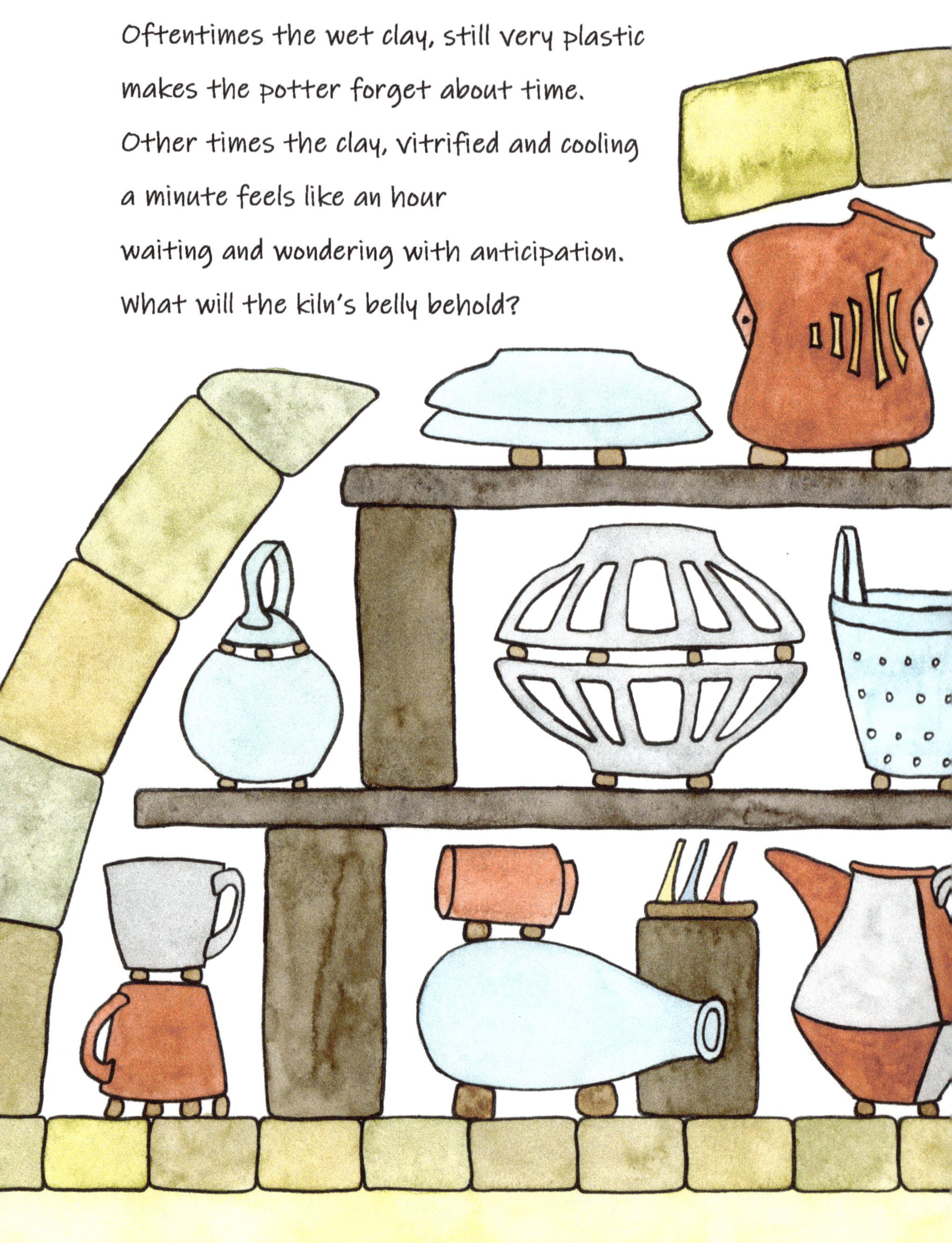

Oftentimes the wet clay, still very plastic
makes the potter forget about time.
Other times the clay, vitrified and cooling
a minute feels like an hour
waiting and wondering with anticipation.
What will the kiln's belly behold?

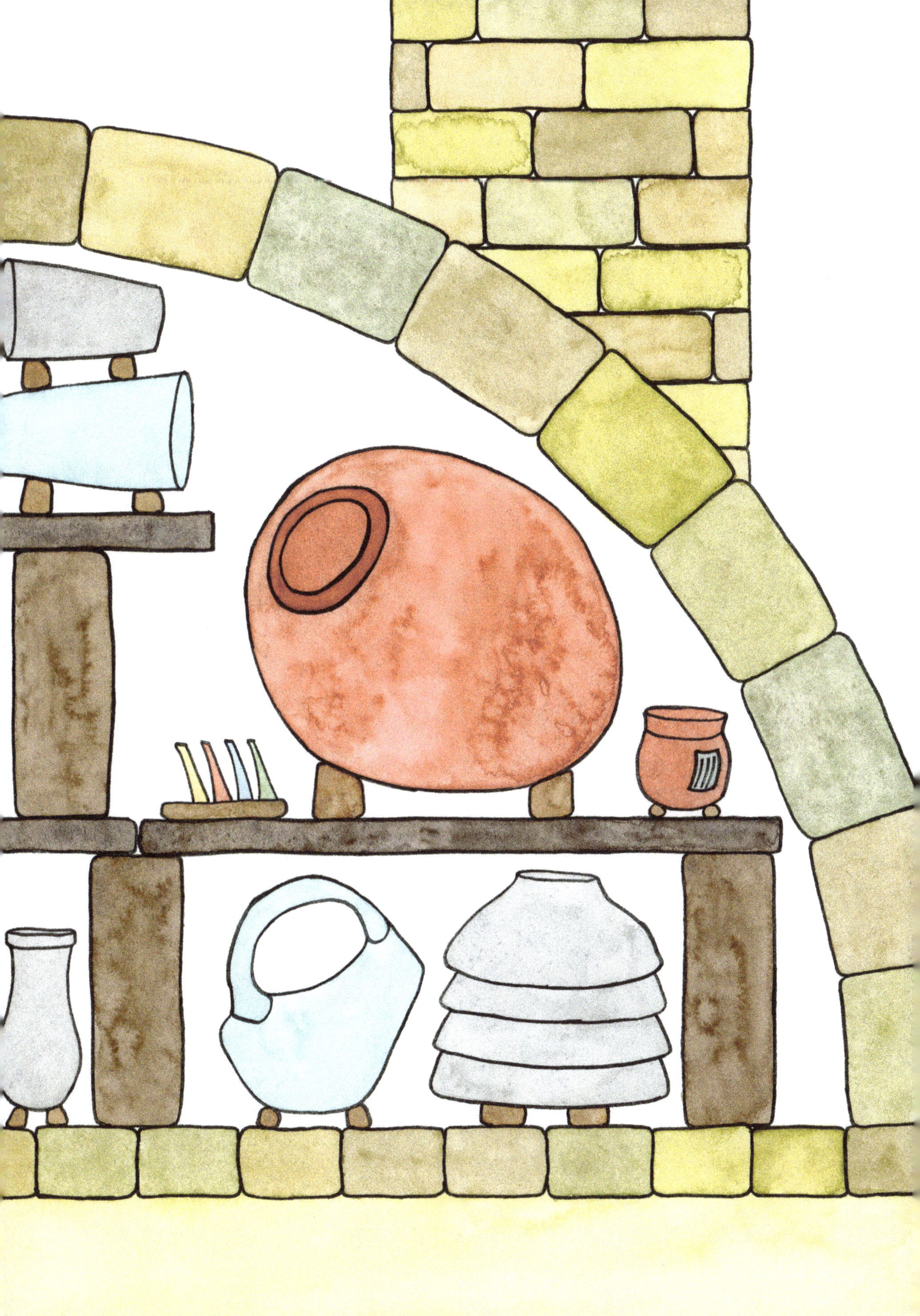

Pottery is nice because you'll have favorite pots.

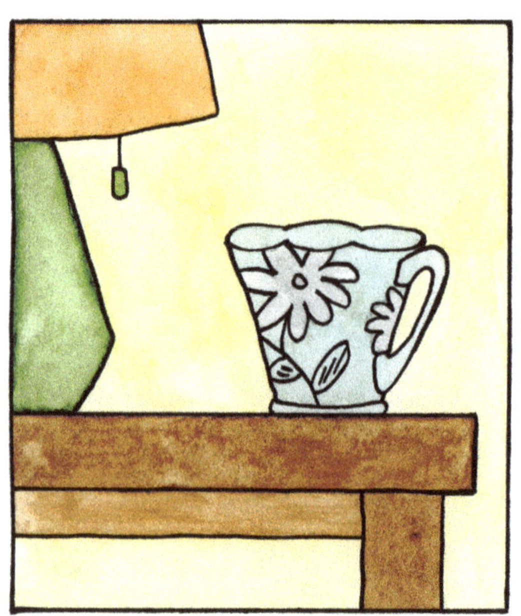

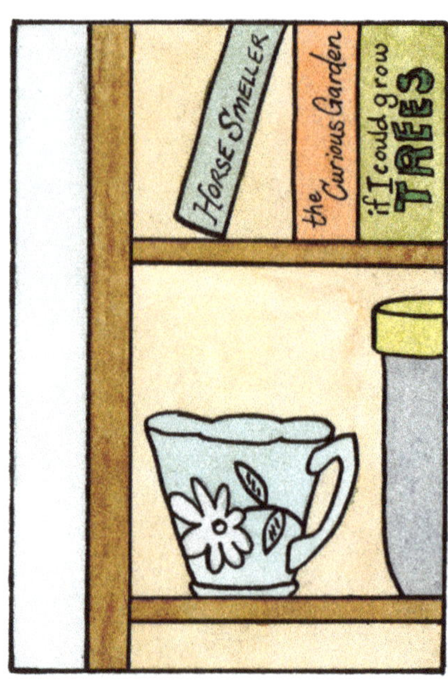

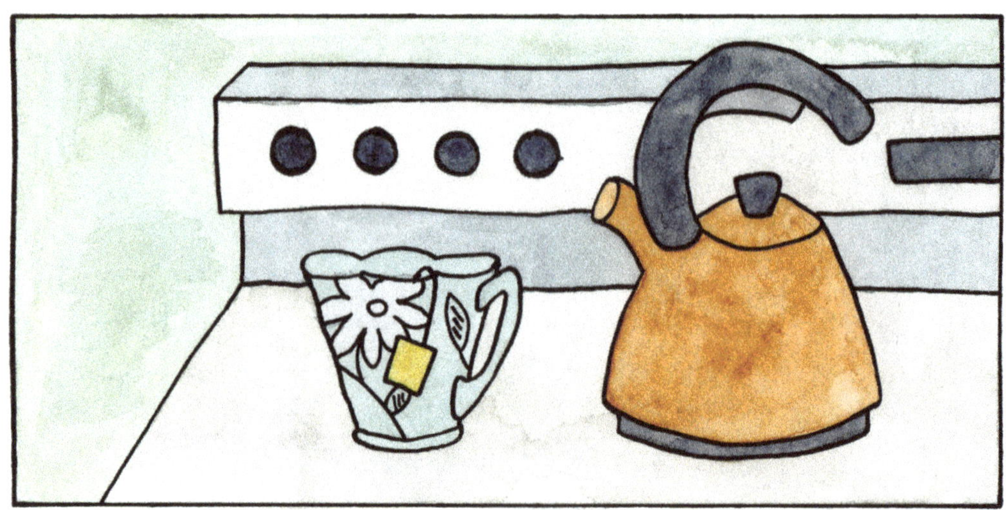

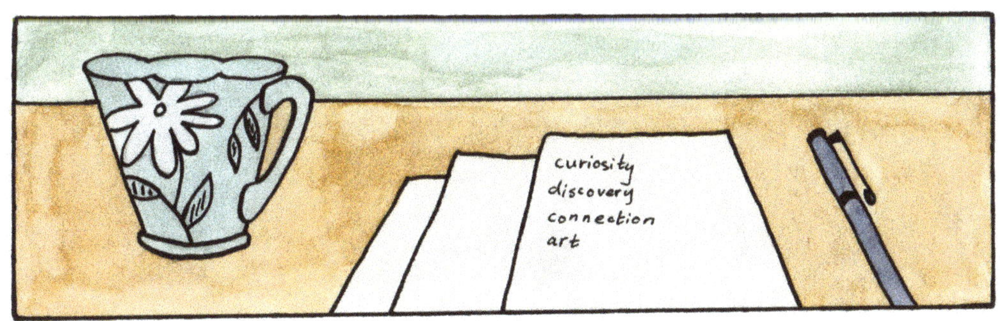

pots holding memories

memories of use

stacking up

first as words

filling up pages

bound into books

books of memories

stories of pottery

vessels holding vessels

filling up shelves

shelves of memories

memories of pots

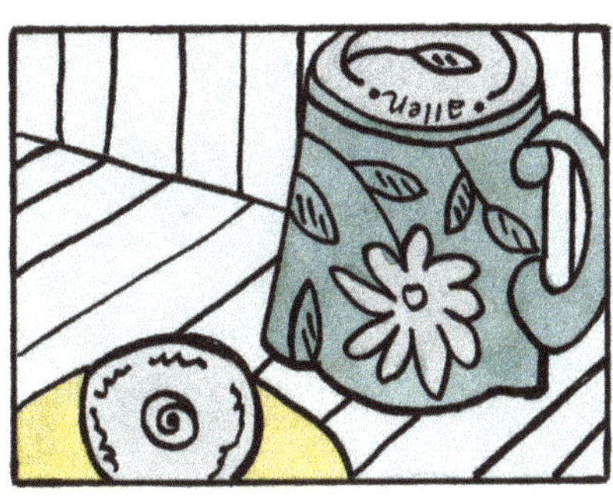

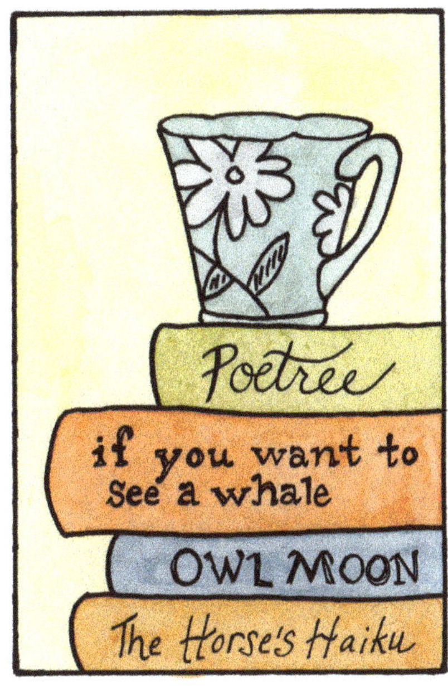

Pottery is about community.

The clay body - generous, giving, kind.

We hold each other's histories.

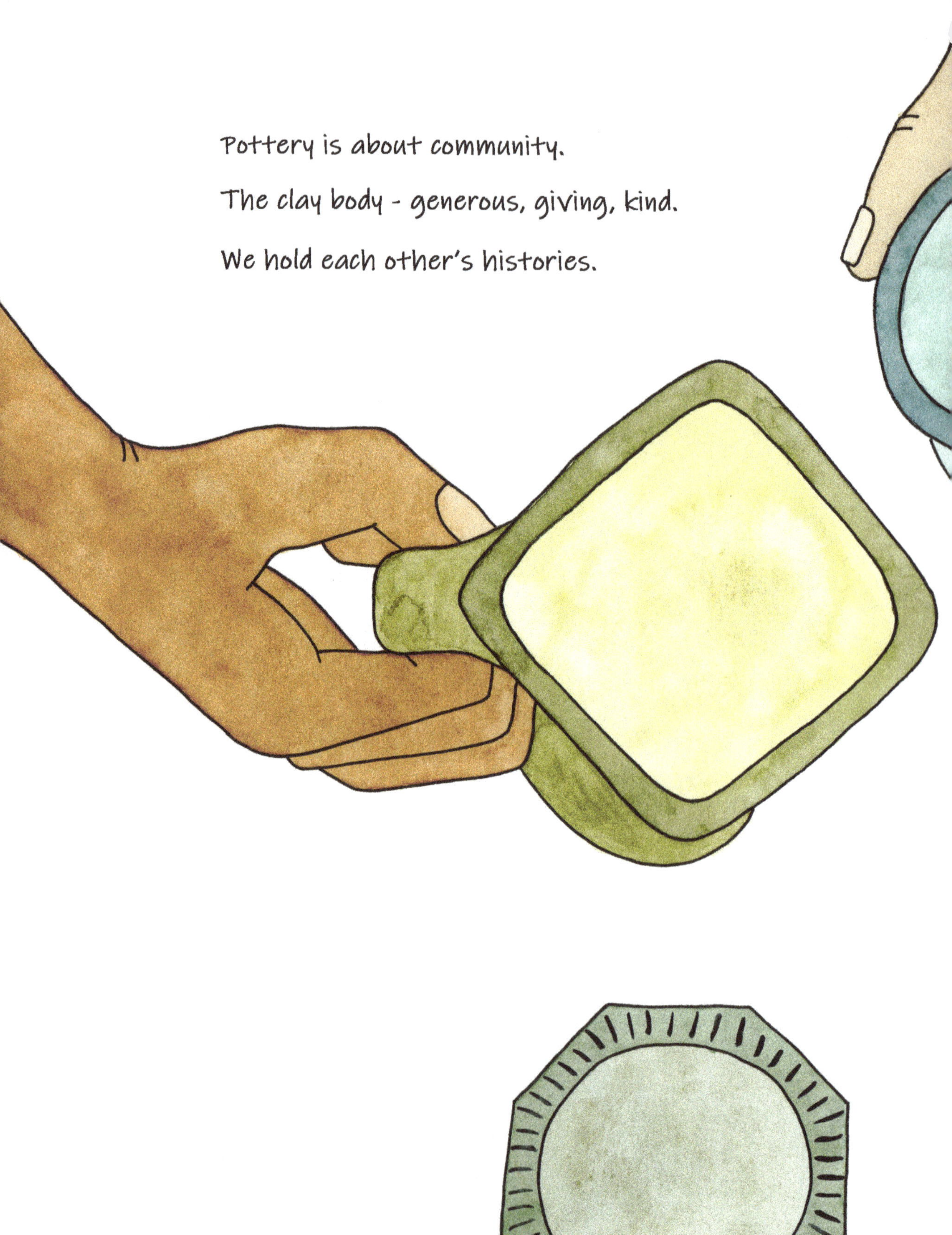

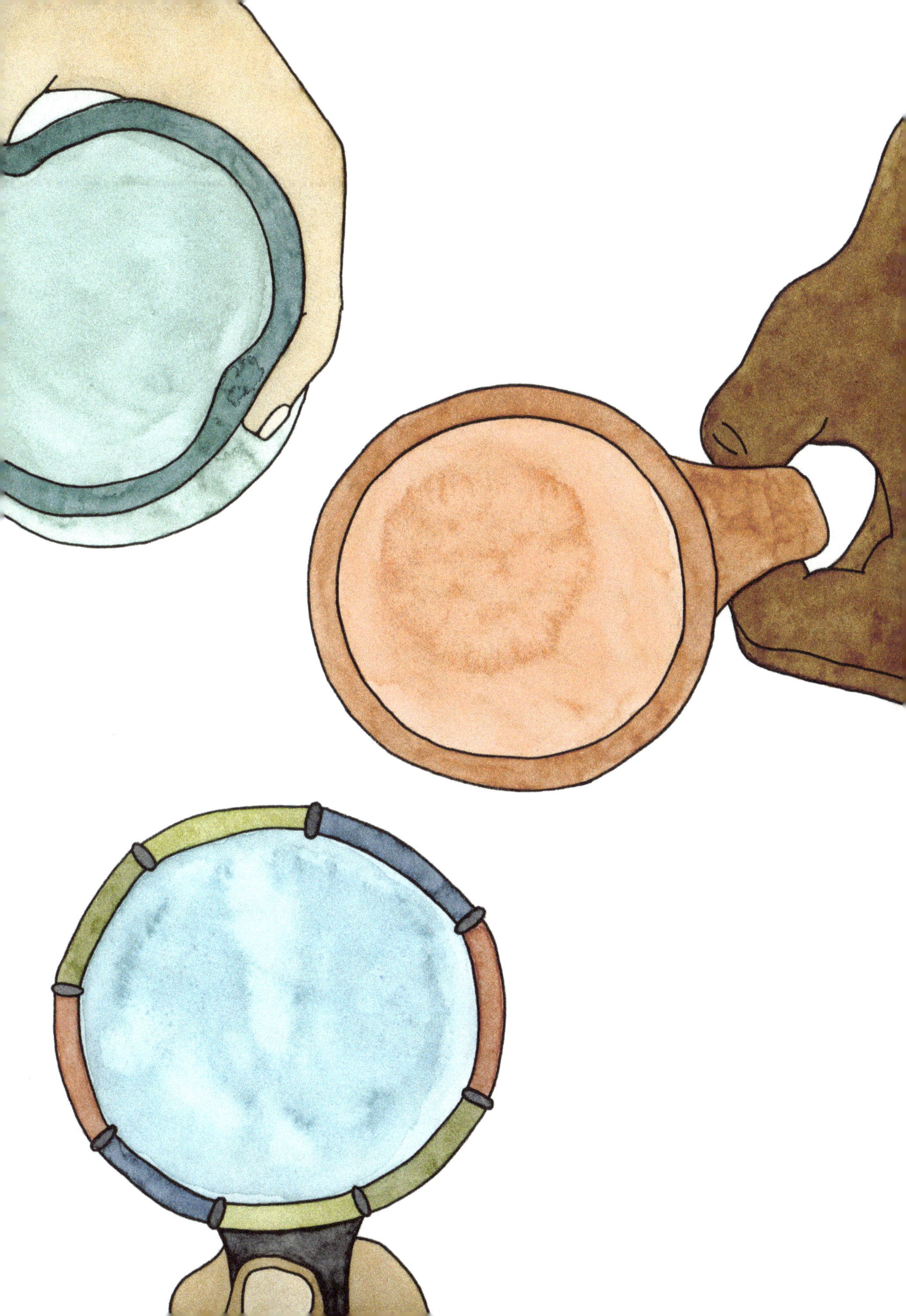

A Place to Start

Potters Featured in Illustrations

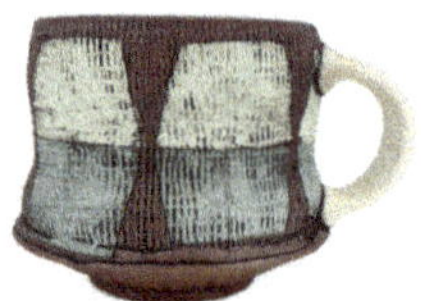

Mark Arnold

MarkArnoldCeramics.com

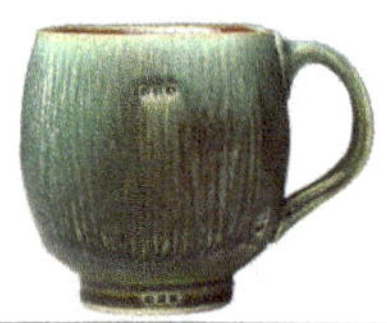

Nick DeVeirs

DeVeirsPottery.com

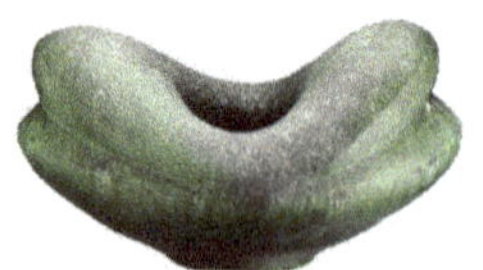

Jerilyn Virden

BorealisStudios.com

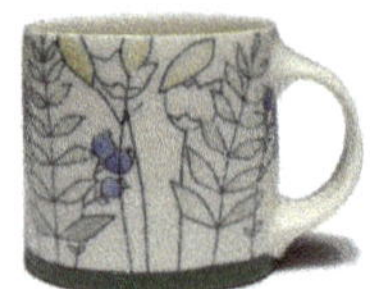

Jenna Vanden Brinks

JennaVandenBrink.com

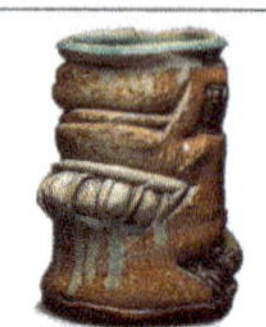

Mark Fehl

TampaTourDeClay.com

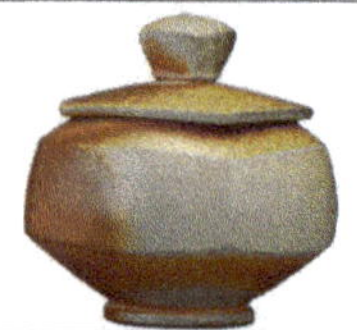

William Baker

WilliamBakerPottery.com

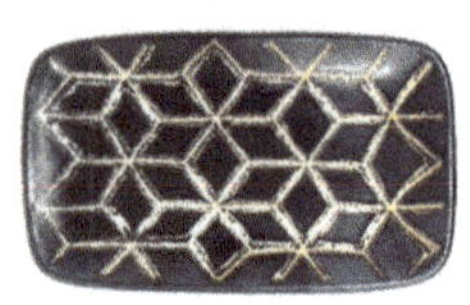

Courtney Martin

CourtneyMartinPottery.com

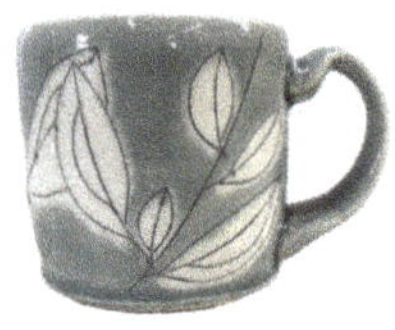

Alyssa Westenbroek-Koster

AWKClayWorks.com

Lorna Meaden

LornaMeadenPottery.com

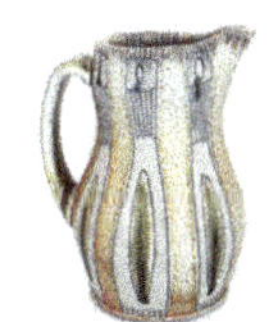

Robbie Lobell

CookonClay.com

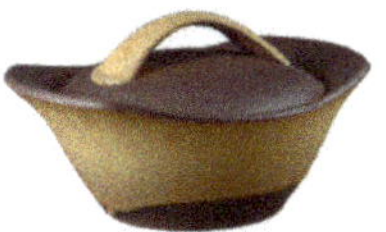

Bill Wilkey

WilkeyArts.com

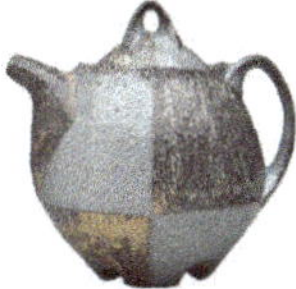

Michael Hunt & Naomi Dalglish

BandanaPottery.com

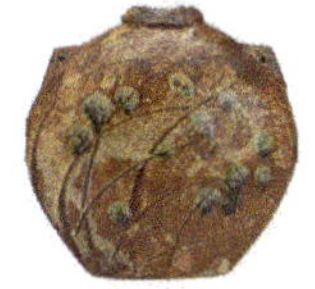

Autumn Higgins

Autumn-Higgins.com

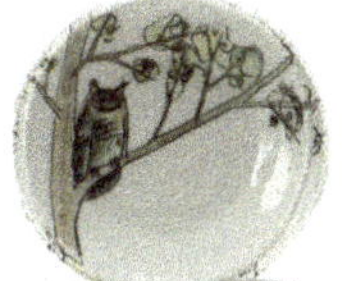

Sarah Pike

SarahPikePottery.com

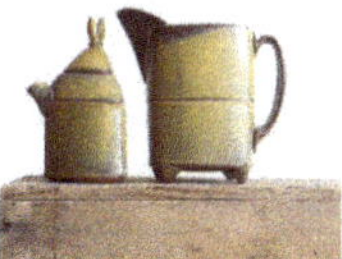

Ben Carter

CarterPottery.com

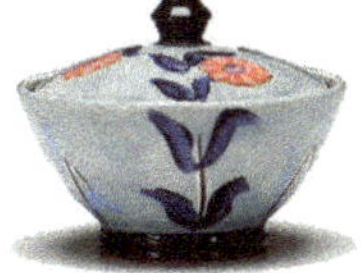

Adam Field

AdamFieldPottery.com

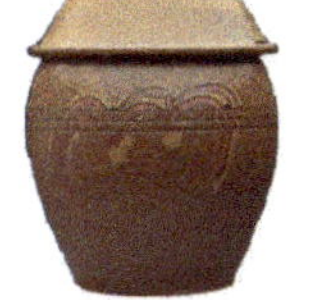

Mckenzie Smith

TampaTourDeClay.com

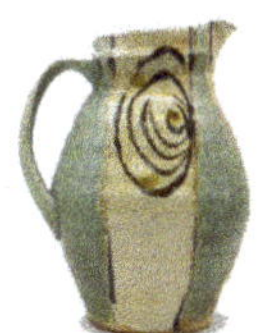

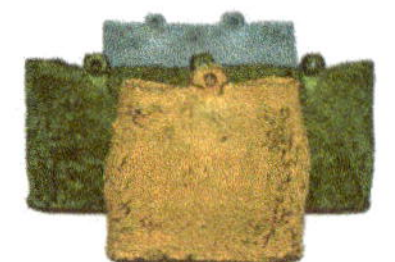

Sunshine Cobb

SunshineCobb.com

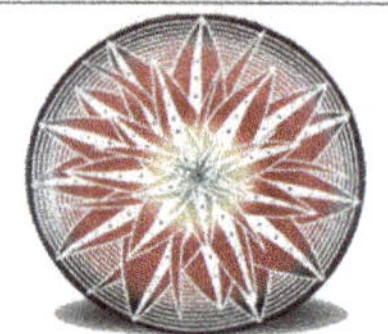

Wayne Bates

WayneBates.com

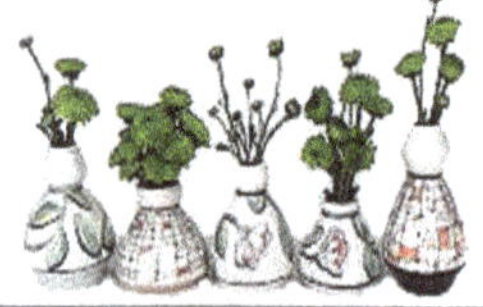

Chandra Debuse

ChandraDebuse.com

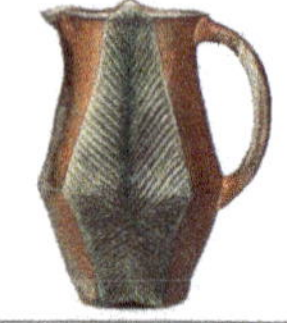

Joy Tanner

JoyTannerPottery.com

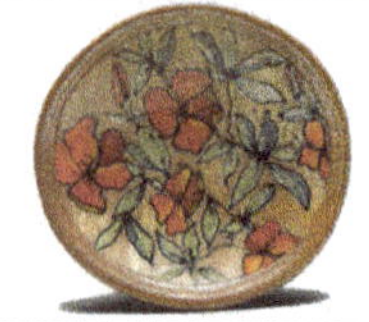

Kim Kirchman

TampaTourDeClay.com

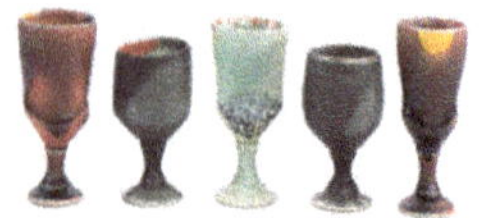

Deb Shwartzkopf

RatCityStudios.com

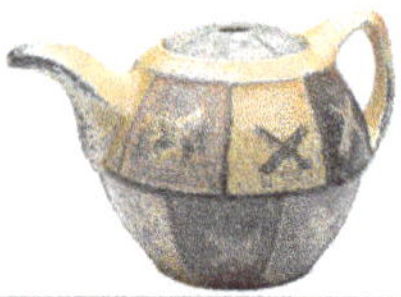

Kenyon Hansen

KenyonMHansen.com

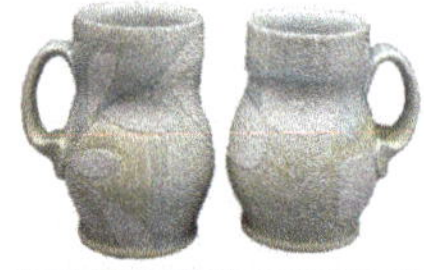

Jennifer Allen

JenniferAllenCeramics.com

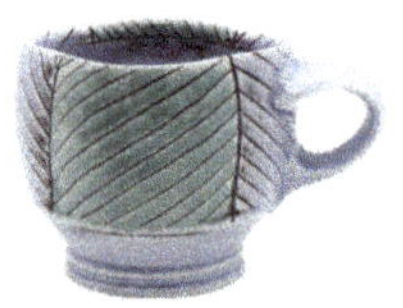

Doug Peltzman

DougPeltzman.com

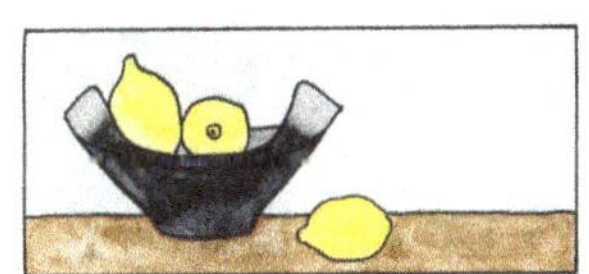 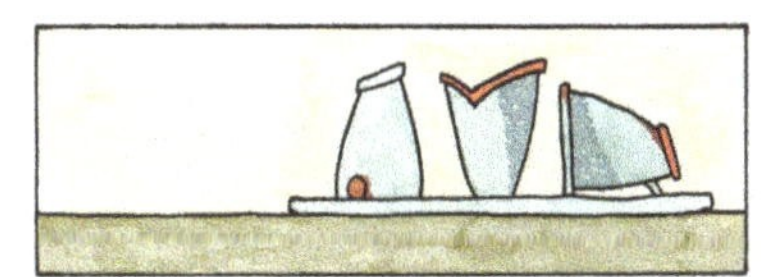 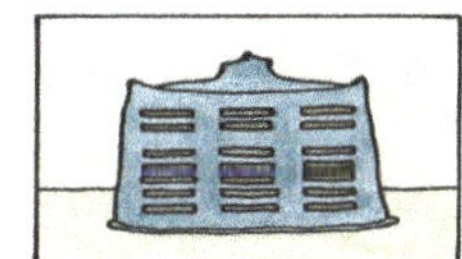

Glossary

Wedge – The process of rolling the clay into a tight spiral, mixing by pressing. Wedging makes the clay more flexible and removes air pockets.

Rib - A wide, flat handheld tool used to shape, smooth and scrape clay surfaces. Ribs are usually made from wood, rubber or metal. They can be rigid or flexible.

Glaze - A mixture of minerals and water that become a glassy surface on the pot after firing. Glazes are applied by dipping, pouring, brushing and spraying.

S Crack - A crack that occurs at the bottom of a pot, in the shape of an "S". Different things can cause an S crack, i.e. when a pot dries unevenly or if the bottom wasn't compressed well during the throwing process.

Vitrified - When clay is heated to a mature temperature it becomes vitrified. The clay's pores seal up and the pot will be able to hold water. Different clays reach vitrification at different temperatures.

Kiln - A furnace (oven) for firing clay. There are electric, gas and wood firing kilns.

Clay body – The clay body is what the clay is made up of, its ingredients. There are thousands of clay bodies, but the main three are porcelain, stoneware and earthenware.

Plastic - If clay is too wet or too dry, it becomes hard to work. When clay is plastic, it can be shaped easily and it is in the ideal state for throwing.